PENGUIN B[...]
THE ESSENTIAL SINDH[...]

Aroona Reejhsinghani is a prolific writer and has contributed extensively to magazines, newspapers and periodicals. She has authored books on diverse subjects including the various regional cuisines of India, and cookbooks for healthy eating. Aroona also develops recipes for a number of multinational companies for their products. Aroona lives in Mumbai with her husband and daughter.

THE ESSENTIAL
SINDHI
COOKBOOK

Aroona Reejhsinghani

PENGUIN BOOKS

PENGUIN BOOKS

Published by the Penguin Group

Penguin Books India Pvt Ltd, 11 Community Centre, Panchsheel Park, New Delhi 110 017, India

Penguin Group (USA), 375 Hudson Street, New York, NY 10014, USA (a division of Penguin Group (USA) Inc.)

Penguin Books (Canada), 10 Alcorn Avenue, Suite 300, Toronto, Ontario M4V 3B2, Canada (a division of Pearson Canada Ltd)

Penguin Books (UK), 80 Strand, London WC2R 0RL, England (a division of Penguin Books Ltd)

Penguin Books (Australia), 250 Camberwell Road, Camberwell, Victoria 3124, Australia (a division of Pearson Australia Group Pty Ltd)

Penguin Group (NZ), cnr Airborne and Rosedale Roads, Albany, Auckland 1310, New Zealand (a division of Pearson New Zealand Ltd)

Penguin Books (South Africa) (Pty) Ltd, 24 Sturdee Avenue, Rosebank 2196, South Africa (a division of Penguin Group (South Africa) (Pty) Ltd)

Penguin Books Ltd, Registered Offices: 80 Strand, London WC2R 0RL, England

First published by Penguin Books India 2004

Copyright © Aroona Reejhsinghani 2004

Illustrations by Subroto Mallick

Typeset in *Perpetua* by Mantra Virtual Services, New Delhi
Printed at Saurabh Printers Pvt. Ltd., A-16, Sector IV, Noida

*I dedicate this book to my late mother Shrimati Thakuri,
a great culinary expert, who initiated me into the art of
cooking. I also dedicate it to my maternal grandfather
Shri Ramkrishin Motwane, a visionary and one of the great
business tycoons of his time.*

Contents

Contents

Introduction

Though Sindh is now in Pakistan, the land was once a part of the great mosaic that was India. The Ramayana and the Mahabharata, the two ancient Indian epics, refer to the land of Sindh and its kings. According to the Ramayana a Sindhi king was part of the royal assembly that had gathered to pay respects to Lord Rama at his naming ceremony. In the Mahabharata the raja of Sindh, Jayadratha, plays an even more central role as he is married to the only sister of the Kauravas and takes part in the eighteen-day war. The Mahabharata also tells us that Lord Krishna's son Samb ruled Sindh, and today some communities of Sindh consider themselves his direct descendants.

Many historians are of the view that Sindhis have their roots in the Harappan civilization. After the Aryans occupied the Indus Valley, their culture, language and religion intermingled with that of the indigenous people and the amalgam produced the people of Sindh.

With the Partition of the Indian subcontinent in 1947, many Sindhis were uprooted from their homeland. Though they have made their homes in different parts of the world, they still feel connected to Sindh. The hopes and aspirations of the children of Sindh, their search for their roots and their desire to know more about their motherland has inspired me to write this book.

I have written it in the hope of keeping the customs and traditions of Sindh alive and the following pages provide a brief glimpse of a bygone era when the people of Sindh were in the land of their birth.

WHO IS A SINDHI

The history of this highly civilized and cultured people goes back over 7000 years to the great Harappan civilization that evolved along the banks of the Sindhu River. The vast river flowing down the plains of Bharatvarsha and its fertile land attracted not only the Aryans who settled down along its banks but also the Turks, Arabs, Sama, Soomars, Kalhoras, Talpurs and finally the British.

During the early Muslim conquests, the people of Sindh were subjected to reckless slaughter and forcible conversions and temples were pulled down. In spite of this, the spirit of Sindhiyat, Sindhi culture, could not be subdued. The spirit of tolerance, cooperation, hospitality and compassion continued to flourish and it inspired many Sindhi Sufi poets like Sachal, Shah Abdul Latiff and Roohal to create lofty and divine kalaams or songs.

The Partition resulted in the migration of Sindhis from their motherland and many of them became refugees. They were scattered across the globe, but wherever they settled they took their customs, culture, festivals, literature and religion with them. They are enterprising, hardworking, industrious and full of faith and courage. Armed with an indomitable faith in God, the noble principles of their saints and seers, and a resolute determination to succeed, they have succeeded in whatever they have undertaken. They have won laurels in the fields of education, medicine, law, science, technology, creative arts and above all philanthropy—building educational institutes, hospitals, dharamshalas, orphanages, temples etc., wherever they settled.

The Sindhis are a cosmopolitan community who transcend all castes and racial, religious and national barriers.

SOME IMPORTANT CITIES OF SINDH

Karachi
Karachi, the capital of Sindh, is to Pakistan what Mumbai is to India, because of its cosmopolitan outlook, its social activities, its modernity and its grandeur, and above all its nearness to the sea. Originally a fishing village, it was called Kalachi, after a beautiful fisherwoman. With the advent of British rule the name was changed to Karachi and this small fishing village became the most important city of Sindh.

The hub of political, social, cultural and commercial sectors of the region, Karachi became famous for its cosmopolitan outlook.

Manahori Island, in the sea off Karachi, was used for trading. It has a temple dedicated to Lord Darya Shah, who is also known as Jhulelal or Uderolal. He is an incarnation of Lord Vishnu and the greatest of all the gods worshipped by Sindhis. Despite being surrounded by the sea, the temple has a sweet-water well, which is considered a miracle by many. Every Sunday thousands of people visited the island to pray at the temple and later enjoy a picnic.

Another famous temple in Karachi is Rataneswar Mahadav in Clifton. Situated in a dark cave below sea level, it is made entirely of marble. It has a lingam of Lord Mahadev in the shape of the zero, indicating that the world is nothing but a dream. This temple too contains a spring of sweet water, which is believed to have many miraculous properties.

Ram Jharokh Lake lies between the hills of Clifton and Manohari Island. It is said that Lord Rama, Sita and Lakshman rested here before starting on their journey to the Himalaya.

Malir, situated about 24 kilometres from the centre of Karachi, has many beautiful gardens and was a famous picnic spot.

Hyderabad

After Karachi, Hyderabad was perhaps the most magnificent city in Sindh. The River Phuleli forms a curve around it. On one side of the river are beautiful, well-laid-out gardens. One of the great attractions in these gardens is a wonderful herb, which is green and fresh throughout the year. Amazingly, if a male touches it, it starts closing its leaves, but if a female touches it, the plant does not react. It was therefore called sharam booti, flower of modesty, and people came from far and wide to see it while also enjoying a picnic in the gardens.

Before Partition Sindhis, like Muslims, observed purdah by covering their faces when venturing out, but the women in Hyderabad were very modern for their times and resisted the purdah system. But this invited the lecherous eyes of the zamindars, who would not hesitate to kidnap or murder to get hold of a woman who caught their fancy. Parents on the other hand thought it wiser to poison their daughters rather than handing them over to the zamindars.

Hyderabad is also famous for its Kali temple on Ganja

Takar, which has a replica of the idol in the Kali temple of Calcutta. Renowned for its beautiful architecture, the temple was a favoured pilgrim centre for Hindus across the subcontinent.

Hirabad

Hirabad was famous for its fashion, beauty, fun and food. The women of this city were also modern in their outlook but many of them remained unmarried because of the great curse of the dowry system. In the liberal environment of Hirabad, young women and men intermingled freely and subsequently there were many love marriages.

The Sindhis of Hirabad had a penchant for showing off, whether they were in a condition to do so or not. Even the poorest ones would keep a servant as a status symbol.

Hirabad was also well known for its food, especially wadi ji machhi (fish roasted in sand) and raan (leg of mutton), and visitors from outside made sure they tasted these delicacies. Then there was the Hirabad lassi made in a special matka or pot of black clay collected from the banks of the river. At a time when most people had never eaten ice cream, and it was not commercially available, Hirabad was famous for its ice cream soda.

Shikarpur

Up to the seventeenth century Shikarpur was covered by thick forests overrun by wild animals and it was the favourite hunting ground of the Mirs, the rulers of Sindh.

Because of its strategic location along the caravan route, a town was set up here in 1617. Trade flourished and as the town's prosperity increased, many hospitals and schools were built and charitable trusts set up.

Shikarpur's Dhak Bazaar was an architectural

wonder. Completely covered by a marvellous wooden canopy, it remained as cool as an air-conditioned chamber even in the hottest of seasons.

The most important place of worship was Khatwari Durbar, built by a Sikh guru.

Sakhar

Like Shikarpur, Sakhar was a famous trading centre. A railway line was laid in 1878, which connected it to all the important towns of Sindh. As a result the city prospered even further and was called the Pride of Sindh.

The most famous landmark here is the Lansdowne Bridge, built in 1889. It was a suspension bridge—the second of its kind, the first being the Golden Gate Bridge in San Francisco. It had sixty gates, each 60 feet long with aluminium doors weighing about 50 tonnes. It was used for heavy traffic entering the city. By its side was another bridge for local traffic, which was five times longer than the famous London Bridge over the Thames.

Larkana

Larkana is still undoubtedly one of the most beautiful cities of Sindh. Adorned with gardens full of different flowers and fruit trees, it is the true inheritor of Sindhi culture and civilization, and was called the Eden of Sindh. The most famous gardens are Gyan Baugh and Tajar Baugh. The mangoes of the latter were so famous that they were regularly sent to the Queen Mother in England.

Larkana's ancient name was Chandaka. It got its present name from a group of sailors called Larak, who migrated to this fertile, beautiful land and established a village here. Larkana attained worldwide fame due to its proximity to Mohenjo-Daro and people from all over visit

Larkana on their way to this great seat of the Harappan civilization.

Hussein and Lal bazaar were the two famous landmarks of Larkana. Women visited these bazaars for clothes and jewellery, and young, eligible bachelors came to eye these beauties. Many a match was made here, thus earning the bazaars the nickname *mehboob jo milan ji jagah* (the place of the beloveds).

Larkana was famous for its pure ghee sweets, guavas and palms. In olden days, everything in Larkana was different, unique and marvellous, and the people were lovers of beauty and nature. Therefore it was said of Larkana:

> *If you have money visit Larkana,*
> *Otherwise keep on wandering lonely.*
> *Larkana is very loveable*
> *Because it is the abode of the beloved.*

Sewhan

Sewhan was originally called Shiv Asthan, the abode of Lord Shiva. The Arabs who came here as conquerors named it Sabasthan, and it was later changed to Sewhan. The area around the city produces the best wheat in Sindh.

The tomb of Lal Shahbaaz Qalander is a place of pilgrimage for both Hindus and Muslims. Lal Shahbaaz Qalander could recite the Koran by heart when he was eight years old. He was always in a state of ecstasy and it was said that gazals flowed from his mouth like sacred springs. He died in 1362 and a magnificent tomb was built in his memory. Every year a fair is held in his honour and singers, dancers and poets gather from all over Sindh to celebrate the event.

Lakley Tirath

Lakley Tirath is a town 18 kilometres south of Sewhan. Nearby is a village called Lakki, which is known for its hot springs. From the top of the mountains steaming hot water flows down and at the foot of the mountains is a cool water fountain. People from all over the country came here to cure skin diseases because these waters were believed to have miraculous curative properties.

Rohri

The ancient city of Rohri was built along the slopes of a mountain. Every street corner here has a tomb of some pir or saint. People still flock to this city because they believe that many of these tombs have the power to cure diseases.

The city was congested and the streets were so narrow that at any time only one-way traffic was allowed.

The most popular landmark of Rohri was the Dhak Bazaar, which is covered by a canopy of wood like the one at Shikarpur.

Basant Panchami was the most popular festival here, and celebrated on a very large scale. People from all over Sindh tried to come here to participate in it.

Thato

Thato is famous because Emperor Shah Jehan lived here before he moved to Delhi. It has innumerable mosques, the largest being the Jama Masjid built by Shah Jehan.

Noor Jam Tamchi

Noor Jam Tamchi is 24 kilometres from Thato and was a place of pilgrimage for young lovers because here lie the tombs of Jam Tamchi and his lovely Queen Noori, who was a fisherwoman by birth. The story, immortalized by Shah Abdul Latiff, tells us how King Jam Tamchi, who had many wives, saw Noori with a group of fishermen and was smitten by her. The next day he announced that he would take a fisherwoman as his wife. All the fisherwomen arrived at court dressed to the hilt except Noori, who was dressed in her usual simple clothes. The king chose her and they were so much in love with each other that they wanted to be buried next to each other.

The people living here were known as Bhatias; they spoke in a distinct dialect and were mainly vegetarians.

SINDHI CEREMONIES

The wedding ceremony
Wedding rites have come down to Sindhis through ancient times and bear the stamp of their rich cultural heritage. The celebrations and ceremonies start ten days before the wedding date. Relatives from all over the world arrive for a wedding. They congregate at the homes of the bride and the groom and the atmosphere is full of mirth and merriment. There is fun and frolic all day, and in the evenings the ladies gather together to dance and sing wedding songs, which are known as laada. Rich and poor are all invited to enjoy the occasion.

In Sindh the rich would invite dancers and singers from places as far away as Calcutta, Lucknow and Lahore to entertain their guests. Marriages were, and even today are, incomplete without the shehnaiwalas playing their melodious tunes. Here are some of the important rites preformed before the wedding ceremony:

Ukharee-mooree-jo-saath

Ukharee-mooree-jo-saath is preformed by both the bride and the groom in their respective homes at exactly the same time according to the muharat (time specified by the priest). They throw pieces of whole turmeric into an ukharee (wooden pot) and break it into small pieces using a mooree (wooden stick), making sure that the turmeric pieces do not fly out of the pot while doing so. This ritual is meant to signify that when either partner faces difficulties in life, they will solve them together without any outsider being aware of it.

Duki-jo-saath

Duki-jo-saath is also performed by the bride and the groom in their own homes at the muharat. Wheat grains are put into a duki (stone grinder) and the bride or the groom, along with seven married women, turn the grinder two to three times to grind the grain. The significance of this ritual is that once they enter married life the couple will share all household responsibilities and stand together solidly like rocks no matter what trials they may have to face.

Tel-jo-saath

During the Tel-jo-saath the bride and the groom offer prayers to Lord Ganesha in their respective homes. After this relatives pour oil on their heads. This signifies that the relatives are pouring good wishes on the bridal pair and pray that they enter married life with a fresh, energetic and practical outlook.

Ghadé-jo-saath

Ghadé-jo-saath is performed by the mothers of the bride and the groom in their respective homes. The mother is made to wear a pink sari and, carrying a ghadi (earthen pot) on her head, she goes to the entrance of her home accompanied by her relatives, some playing the dholak. The mother, who had till then been loaded with the responsibility of bringing up her child, is now relieved of her responsibility and she prays that married life will bring happiness and prosperity to her child.

Dhakni-jo-saath
The bride and groom are made to wear new shoes and with one stroke are asked to break the dhakni (cover) of an earthen pot to prove their strength.

Tearing of old clothes
The bride and the groom after completing all these rituals go to seek the blessings of their elders and then they go to the youngsters in the family, who tear off their old clothes. From this day on they should forget their old lives and start a new life together.

The wedding day
On the wedding day, the groom is given a bath by his mother after massaging his body with a mixture of oil, turmeric and multani mitti (fuller's earth). His mother and sister tie a thread in his hair, put kaajal or surma in his eyes and butter or honey in his mouth. Then, accompanied by the recitation of slokas by a Brahmin, the groom and his parents are garlanded and honoured with pink dupattas by their relatives. The groom rides a mare and is accompanied by his sister and brother-in-law. The procession is led by the baratis (the members of the groom's party) and shehnai players. The baratis dance

and sing all the way to the wedding venue, while the elders throw coins over the groom. When the procession reaches the bride's home they are welcomed with papad and sherbet.

The mother of the bride performs the aarti or blessing over the groom and she washes his feet in a thali of milk. The bride is then brought to the gate and they are allowed a glimpse of each other through a see-through curtain. The Brahmin ties the hand of the bride to that of the groom with a thread as a sign of the groom's readiness to accept the bride. The wedding ceremony is then performed and takes six to eight hours to complete.

After the wedding

After the wedding ceremony is completed, a grand welcome awaits the bride at her in-laws' home. While entering the home she carries an earthen pot on her head from which she sprinkles milk all the way in, to indicates that like the goddess Lakshmi she will bring prosperity and plenty into the home. After this she is made to go through the salt-measuring ceremony, where each family member exchanges a handful of salt with her. The ritual suggests that as salt gets mixed into everything, so too the bride will get along with every member of the family. In the last ritual she has to remove as many silver coins as she can from a pot of milk in one stroke. This is supposed to indicate her skill and patience in handling household affairs.

The bedroom is lavishly and beautifully decorated with garlands of fragrant flowers. A coconut and a glass of milkshake made with plenty of dry fruits and saffron is placed near the bed. The groom breaks the coconut and drinks the milk to signify that he will care for the physical and emotional well-being of his bride.

Mundan ceremony
The mundan ceremony is performed on the male child between the ages of three months to one year. A goat without any blemish is sacrificed on the day. It is skinned and the meat is separated from the bones very carefully so that none of the bones are broken. The meat is made into various dishes and served to relatives and friends who attend the ceremony.

A barber is invited to shave the hair of the child, which is then wrapped in the goat's skin and buried either at the burial ground or at the threshold of the house. The popular belief is that the contents of the skin will rise up in the form of a horse to carry the child to paradise on the day of resurrection.

Amongst the bhaibands (the professional Sindhis) the maternal grandparents gift yellow clothing to the child along with various other gifts.

Thread ceremony
The thread ceremony is a very important event in the life of a Sindhi boy. It is performed by a Brahmin in the presence of the boy's parents, family and friends before he reaches puberty. The child's head is shaved; he is given a bath and is made to wear a dhoti. Then as a mark of the child's initiation into the religion, the Brahmin makes him wear the janaiya or sacred thread. It consists of three strings which are twisted together. They symbolize the three forms of the one Supreme Being: Brahma the Creator, Vishnu the Preserver and Shiva the Destroyer. It also

symbolizes the three duties he has to perform in life: towards his parents and ancestors, towards society and towards his own spiritual development and knowledge of truth. The knot in the thread symbolizes control over mind and senses and the twist symbolizes honesty. The thread is a reminder to him that he should keep himself clean of all impurities like hatred, jealousy, envy, anger, disappointment, humiliation and sadness.

On this occasion a yajna is preformed where all the gods are invoked to provide a healthy life and a sharp intellect to the child. The Brahmin then pours water over the folded palms of the child to purify him and then he is given the Gayatri Mantra. (The Gayatri Mantra invokes the sun god and when recited early morning in the sun is believed to bring the mind and body into harmony.) The ceremony ends with the relatives and friends giving gifts to the child.

A large banquet consisting of vegetarian dishes is held and there is plenty of food, fun and frolic.

Shradh ceremony
In September, soon after Ganesh Chaturthi and before Dussera, comes the Shradh. During Shradh no Sindhi undertakes auspicious work. Shradh is performed for the solace of the soul of a departed ancestor. On the day of the Shradh Brahmins are called in and a pooja and a havan are performed after which they are given gifts of money and clothes. Special food which was the ancestor's favourite is prepared on that day and first given to crows. If the crows do not eat the food it is supposed to be an indication that the ancestor is not happy with the offerings. Once the food has been offered to the crows, the Brahmins are fed and then the family can eat.

SINDHI FESTIVALS

Tirmoori

Tirmoori, called Makar Sankranti in western India, arrives in January. It is believed that on this day the moon starts moving from the north to the south, while the sun starts its northward journey, coming closer to us and bringing us its warmth. This day is called Tirmoori or Datraan. The Mahabharat says that Bhishma Pitamah waited for this auspicious day lying on his bed of arrows to breathe his last because it is considered propitious even in devlok where the gods reside. On this day parents send ladoos and chikki made of sesame seeds (tirr) to their daughters' homes, hence the name Tirmoori.

Shivratri

Shivratri falls in February and is celebrated with great fervour by Sindhis. People get up early in the morning, take a bath, wear new clothes and visit Lord Shiva's temple with offerings of milk, fruits and bael patra, which are believed to be great favourites of Lord Shiva. Offerings are made to the poor and needy. The diet is restricted to specific foods like potato, sago and poories made of water chestnut flour. They drink thadal, made with milk, dry fruits and bhang (fresh cannabis), supposedly the favourite drink of Lord Shiva. The next day the fast is broken with a prasad called kuti (a form of dry halva). On this day, Lord Shiva is popularly believed to awaken from his great samadhi and people try to appease him so that he may listen to their prayers.

Holi

Holi is celebrated in March throughout India. Legend has it that Prahlad's devotion to Lord Vishnu so angered his demon father Hirnyakeshap that he plotted with his sister Holika to burn him alive. Holika was blessed with a dupatta which would save her from fire. However just as the pile of wood on which she was seated with Prahlad on her lap was set aflame, a great wind caused the dupatta to fall on Prahlad, saving him and leaving Holika unprotected. Holi is preceded by the burning of bonfires, signifying the burning of Holika and the triumph of good over evil. The next day people start visiting each other from early morning and spray each other with coloured powders and water, particularly gulal or vermilion red. On Holi too, people drink thadal, and intoxicated, they play the dholak and sing folksongs. There is a lot of fun and merriment, and on this day every Sindhi eats gheear, a sort of jallebi which is sold at Sindhi sweetmeat shops.

Chetichand

Chetichand is one of the most important Sindhi festivals and heralds the Sindhi New Year. It falls in March and celebrates the birthday of Lord Jhulelal, or Uderolal as he was affectionately called. It is a most colourful and impressive festival. A huge procession is taken out at the centre of which is a large colourfully decorated van carrying the idol of Lord Jhulelal, a kalash containing holy water and the Behrana Sahib (a cone-shaped image made of flour and decorated with cloves, cardamoms, betel nuts, sugar candy and turmeric powder), garlanded with fragrant flowers. Incense sticks are burnt and candles and diya are lit, giving a wondrous touch to the atmosphere.

Many tableaux are carried in the procession, which highlight topical burning problems of the society and the country.

The atmosphere is charged with gaiety and reverberates with the sound *ayo lal Jhulelal*. People dance the jhumir and chej (the Sindhi dances performed during weddings and other ceremonies) to the melodious tunes of the shehnai and dholak. The procession terminates at the river ghats which are beautifully decorated and illuminated for the occasion. A prasad of tahri (a sweet rice preparation) is given to all present. Then with the immersion of the offerings and singing of hymns the festival comes to an end.

Akhiteej

Akhiteej is celebrated in May in honour of goddess Parvati and is observed by married women for the long life of their husbands. Fresh water is kept in earthenware pots in the moonlight and the next day all the members of the family drink it. The poor, weary and thirsty are offered water at every nook and corner of the cities; some even offer cold drinks containing pieces of apples and other fruits. It was also customary to send new earthenware pots and fruits to priests in the temples and gurdwaras.

Janmashtami

Janmashtami, the birthday of Lord Krishna, falls in August. Temples across the country create beautifully crafted cradles decorated with garlands of dry fruits, spices and fragrant flowers for this ceremony. Devotees fast till midnight before the idol of baby Krishna, which is kept in the flower-decked cradle. At the stroke of midnight, when the great lord was born, devotional songs known as kirtans are sung in his praise. The singing lasts till morning when people are given burfi and peda (sweetmeats) to break their fast.

Teejri

Teejri is celebrated in August. Women fast for the entire day for the long life, happiness and prosperity of their husbands. Even unmarried girls fast on this day in the hope of getting a good husband. The festival is celebrated in honour of goddess Parvati, who is worshipped on this day. The fast begins at four in the morning, when the women get together and partake of some food. On sighting the moon, the women break the fast with khirni, a sweet dish made of milk, dry fruits and ground rice. Henna is applied on hands and feet in intricate designs and the women spend the day playing games, swinging on swings and singing love songs.

Thadree

Thadree is celebrated a day before Janmashtami. On this day goddess Shitladevi, an avatar of goddess Parvati, is worshipped. Thadree means cold, and no Sindhi lights a fire in the house during this festival. Water is sprinkled on the kitchen fire to appease the goddess, as she dislikes anything hot. The food for the day is prepared the previous day and eaten cold. Sweet and savoury koki (roti) made of gram flour or whole-wheat flour, sweet tikki and a special curd cocktail called matho are prepared. Members of the family gather together and exchange gifts. Card playing sessions are held amid much merriment and enjoyment.

Diwali

Diwali is celebrated in October–November. It is the festival of lights and no matter how poor one may be a diya is lit in every home. 'When the sun and the moon have both set, what light does a person have in the darkness? The fire,' say the Upanishads. There is total darkness on the night of Diwali, and tradition says that on this night a mystic light like the flame of a single lamp shines in the heart of the moon. This flame guides Mahalakshmi, the goddess of wealth, in her descent to earth to bless the humans whose homes are well lit with lamps. Therefore lamps are kept burning all night. This festival celebrates the return of Lord Rama to Ayodhya after defeating the demon Ravana.

Diwali starts with Dhantirus, when people buy new utensils. The second day is Roop Chaturdasi when everyone purifies the body with an oil bath, and the goddess Lakshmi is worshipped along with Ganesha. Coins of gold and silver are immersed in a mixture of curd, milk and honey and offered to the goddess along with a lotus and dhurva grass. After the Lakshmi pooja the coins are reverently touched by each member of the family with their lips while sending up a silent prayer—mother, banish poverty and give us plenty. This is followed by a family dinner, when only vegetarian food is served. Gifts are exchanged, plenty of dry fruits and sweets are eaten and firecrackers are burst. Sindh being an agricultural land, cattle are considered a source of great wealth and the third day of Diwali cows are worshipped during the Goverdhan pooja. Their sheds are coloured with sindoor (vermilion powder), their feet are adorned with anklets and garlands of shells are wound around their necks. On the last day of Diwali, people perform behrana, a dance, accompanied by devotional songs in praise of Lord Jhulelal, who is taken out with great pomp and glory. Earthen lamps are set afloat in the river or the sea and prayers are sent up for the well-being of the universe.

THE SINDHI RELIGION

Sindhi Hindus offer prayers to the Hindu pantheon of gods like Lord Brahma, Vishnu and Mahesh. They also pray to the elements like air, fire, water and sun. But among the Sindhi Hindus is a popular sect known as the Daryapanthies, followers of the River Sindhu, with Jhulelal as their patron saint.

Sindh was conquered by the Arabs and it was ruled by Murkh, who oppressed the Hindus and forcibly converted many of them to Islam. Many lost their lives, and the rest were powerless to do anything. Legend has it that one day in AD 1007 they gathered on the banks of the River Sindhu and fasted and prayed continuously for the next three days. The great lord took pity on their plight and out of the river emerged Lord Vishnu riding a huge fish. He assured the assembled people that after seven days he would be born in human form as their protector. True to the prophecy the divine child was born on the Friday evening of the new moon in the month of Chaitra (April) to a Rajput called Ratan Rai Lhana and his wife Devki in the village of Khanpur. The baby was named Uday Chandra but he was called Uderolal. Women from the village would take turns swinging his cradle while singing a lullaby *Jhulelal muhinjo hindoran mein jhule*, meaning 'my dearest son swings in the cradle (jhula)'. Jhulelal thus became his pet name. Murkh tried his best to harm the young Jhulelal, but his miraculous powers converted the mighty king and he became a great devotee. The deity is also called Jinda Pir or Khawaja Khizir and is greatly revered by Muslims. There is a samadhi of Jhulelal known as Zinda Pir in Nassarpur in Pakistan where both Hindus and Muslims go on pilgrimage. Even today a portion of the interior of the dargah is maintained by sadhus for the worship of Hindu devotees. Prayers are offered day and night here, and there is a thanksgiving festival on Chetichand, which marks the birth of Uderolal.

Some Sindhi Hindus also follow the teachings of the Sikh religion. Up to 1712 the prominent faiths were Hinduism and Buddhism. With the Islamic invasions many were converted to Islam, and later followed the teachings of Guru Nanak, the founder of the Sikh religion. The Sikhs, like the Hindus, resisted the Muslim invaders, which brought the two close to each other. By the time the British arrived in Sindh, the land was flourishing with Sufi mystics, gurus, mullahs and priests. Everyone co-existed side by side peacefully participating in each other's religious ceremonies and living like brothers. Most people were equally comfortable in mosques, gurdwaras and temples. But with Partition, the Sindhis too were divided along religious lines.

SINDHI DANCE AND FOLK SONGS

The dancing girls of Mohenjo-Daro stand testimony to the love of dance and music among the Sindhis. Sindhi dances include jhumir, dhamal, dandia, talli and jhamelo and their music forms are laada, bhagat, dohiraa, kafi and kalaam. Sindhi music is akin to Arab music in rhythm, tune and melody. The music of the two lands is so similar that it is often difficult to differentiate one from the other.

The Samma and Sooma dynasties once ruled over Sindh (though their origin is lost in antiquity), and the famous stories of Moomal–Mahindra, Leela–Chanesar, Umar–Marvee, Noor–Jam Tamchi were immortalized in poetry that was recited and sung by wandering bards, minstrels and bhagats for many centuries. These ballads form the most valuable part of the cultural heritage of Sindh. The Leela–Chanesar ballad, for example, is woven around the story of Princess Kumroo who was so obsessed by Prince Chanesar, who was happily married to Leela, that she comes to serve Leela as a maidservant. She gets to learn of Leela's weakness for jewellery and entices her into giving up Chanesar for a beautiful diamond necklace. By the time Leela realizes her mistake, Chanesar is married to Kumroo and refuses to take her back. Leela returns disguised as a dancing girl. She dances so beautifully and sings such a heart-rending song that Chanesar ultimately takes her back.

The language, literature and culture of the Muslims who invaded and ruled Sindh were influenced by Iran and these influences were felt in Sindh as well, resulting in a blending of cultures. The Sindhi language acquired Iranian vocabulary and the music imbibed Iranian phraseology, but without losing its character.

Sindhi music was standardized by the great Sindhi poet Shah Abdul Latiff. It is unique to Sindh and cannot be found in any other part of the subcontinent.

One of the most famous forms of original Sindhi dance and music is the bhagat. Days in advance there would be an announcement of a bhagat performance and people came from far and near to watch it. The performance usually started at night and lasted till the early hours of the morning. Only men were allowed to perform the bhagat. Two or more performers interacted to weave folktales in song. The lead singer, called the bhagat, would be dressed in jamo (a long coat), pagadi (headgear), chher (anklets) and kundal (earrings) with a red tilak on his head. The backup singers usually stood behind the bhagat. The bhagat would start by singing a line and the backup singers would interject with a simile or the latter half of the couplet. The backup singers were usually dressed as women and were addressed by the bhagat by female names. The bhagat was a hugely popular form of entertainment during festivals, marriages and fairs held in temples and dargahs. The king of the bhagats was Sant Kanwaram, who was a very famous saint revered by Hindus and Muslims alike.

Jhumir was a dance performed by women while singing the laada or wedding songs. No wedding was complete without these songs. The dances were performed a day before the wedding. Relatives and friends were invited to a grand party to witness the jhumir and laada and to show their appreciation, they showered the performers with coins.

Chej was performed by men. It is akin to dholak ras, the famous folk dance of Kathiawar. Music is played on the shehnai and dholak.

Another dance form was the dhamal which was performed mainly by fakirs and Sufi saints. It was characterized by religious fervour and had a very fast tempo. Nagaro, a large drum, provided the beat and tempo for the dance.

Then there is Hajmalo, which is performed during the bherano of Lord Jhulelal. The rhythmic beat and enchanting vitality of these dances and music transport the audiences to another world.

THE CRAFTS OF SINDH

Sindh was famous for its arts and crafts. Craftsmen were held in high esteem and their works were famous not only in Sindh but also in many places abroad.

Pottery

The pottery was breathtakingly beautiful. Vessels were painted with the colours of the rainbow and then glazed with earth called channioh which imparted lustre and brightness to the finished products. These vessels were used for both decorative and cooking purposes.

Some of the most famous and delicious dishes were cooked in stone vessels known as kuni, and kuni ja bhien (lotus stems cooked in a kuni) was a popular snack.

Weaving

The weavers of Sindh produced some of the best bedspreads, lungis and mats in India. The bedspreads had beautiful colours and designs woven into them. The yarn was spun by the women who dyed it and the men worked the loom. Cotton and silk threads were used in bright colours. They were reversible, each side having a different pattern.

Lungis were made of silk, cotton and wool, in both bright and soft colours with beautifully woven broad borders of silver and gold thread.

Mats were used for prayers by Muslims, and by Hindus to sleep on. These too were made in bright colours, popular with both communities. A coarse rug was also produced with goat's hair.

Ajrak

Ajrak was peculiar to Sindh. In this procedure the cloth was first washed in a solution of water and crushed ajrak berries. It was then steamed and stamped with wooden blocks injected with dyes. The printed cloth was then dipped in a solution of indigo and washed in water, when the colours became dazzlingly bright.

Appliqué

Appliqué was a domestic craft women practised when they were free from household duties. Small pieces of different coloured cloth were joined together painstakingly and made into beautiful clothing. It took months to produce them but the end product was something to die for.

Jhandi or lacquer work

Almost all the material for Sindhi craftsmen came from the River Indus. The wood from the trees on its bank was used for carvings and furniture beautifully decorated with lacquer work. The object was coated with a fine powder and polished. Traditional designs were outlined with paint and filled with bright and beautiful colours. After they dried they were varnished with shellac. A swing called pingah, sofas, chairs, vases and lamps were some of the famous items made in jhandi.

Embroidery

Sindhi women excelled in needlework. The thin bronze needles from the excavations of Mohenjo-Daro are witness to this craft. They made fantastic patterns of rich, brilliant colours gleaming with mirrors, shells and beads. Zardosi, a special type of embroidery with a silver or golden thread, was also very famous throughout Sindh.

Leatherwork

The Sindhi tanner was a great master of his craft. He used mangrove and other bark for curing, dying and oiling, and perfected the fine technique of converting crude hide and skin into soft and durable leather shoes which were covered with beautiful designs worked in gold, silver and coloured thread.

HOW SINDHIS GOT THEIR SURNAMES

The surname of a Sindhi family comes from its ancestors. From these surnames it is very easy to track down a Sindhi family tree. All Sindhi surnames are based on their ancestors' names except the Shahanies, who are named after Shah Baro, a beloved chieftain of Larkana.

A sociological study by Bherumal Meharchand shows that Sindhis with the surnames Mukhi, Nagrani, Sagrani, Jethmalani, Lakhani, Lulla, Chabria and Matta are cousins. So are those with the surnames of Advani, Sitlani, Sadwani, Shamdasani and Chandiramani.

The gotar or lineage of Bhambhani, Karnani and Kriplani is Chugh. The gotar of Thadani, Gehani and Raisinghani is Khangar, while the gotar of Chainani, Hingorani and Jaisinghani is Pahuja, and that of Keswani, Ambwani, Mulchandani and Bhagwanani is Kukreja. They are all related to Ajwani, Bhavnani, Gidwani and Jagtiani, and so are Mirchandani, Mehtani, Moorjani, Sadarangani and Makhija.

Sindhis also took on the names of the cities they lived in. Thus a Sindhi from Shikarpur was known as Shikarpuri, from Hyderabad as Hyderabadi, from Sukhur as Sakhru and so on.

Sindhis are divided into two groups—the amils who

were business people and the bhaibands who were in service or were professionals.

SINDHI CUISINE

Hills and dales, rivers and lakes, and undulating green fields make up the landscape of Sindh. Because it was very fertile it attracted a large number of invaders, many of whom influenced the cuisine.

The Muslim invasions resulted in Iranian influences on the cuisine, and many Sindhis started relishing non-vegetarian food. Kabab, raan (leg of mutton) and biryani became the norm. Sindhis not only ate non-vegetarian food for lunch and dinner, they even ate it at breakfast. Their most famous breakfast is kabab with roti and tariyal machhi (fried fish) with phulko (roti).

When Guru Nanak visited Shikarpur, many Sindhis adopted Sikhism and this also influenced Sindhi cuisine. The koki and phulko were the standard Sindhi roti till then, but after the advent of Sikhism bharyal phulko (stuffed parathé) and plain parathé were introduced. A variety of pulses, lentils and non-vegetarian dishes were absorbed from Punjabi cuisine and adapted to their taste. The panchratni dal and tridali are examples of dishes adapted from Punjabi cuisine.

Sindhi cuisine accepted these foreign influences, while still maintaining its own character. Some of these dishes are unique to Sindh. Kuni ja bhien, for example, was sold at every street corner. Another popular dish unique to Sindh was wadi ji machhi.

Fish is a regular part of Sindhi diet, but only fresh water or river fish is eaten, with palo (bhing or hilsa) being the favourite. Pomfret, surmai (kingfish) and other sea fish started gaining popularity after the Sindhis migrated to India. Prawns are the only crustaceans eaten by Sindhis.

All Sindhis are not non-vegetarians. Some are pure vegetarians and some do not even touch garlic and onion. This is probably due to the climate and geographical situation of their homeland. The climate of Sindh was such that bountiful crops of a variety of vegetables were produced all year round. This made it possible for people to exclude non-vegetarian food completely. Vegetables of all types are overwhelmingly popular in Sindhi cuisine and the infinite variety of vegetarian dishes surpasses the best of non-vegetarian dishes in taste and appearance.

HELPFUL HINTS

- **To prepare fish:** Rub it inside and out with turmeric powder, salt and lime juice or vinegar. Set aside for 30 minutes and rinse. This removes the fishy smell. Soak freshwater fish for 30 minutes in salt water to remove any muddy taste and provide the salt it lacks.

- **To cook brains:** Soak it in salt water for 15 minutes, remove its membranes, then boil in water to which a little lime juice or vinegar has been added. The acid helps to keep the meat white and enhances its taste considerably.

- **To prepare lotus stems:** Remove the mud coating with a blunt knife and wash well. Cut it into thick slices at a slant, remove any mud present inside the holes with a toothpick and wash in 2-3 changes of water. Boil in water to which a pinch of sodium bicarbonate and salt have been added, till tender. Drain and use according to the recipe you are following.

- **To make your own mango powder:** Buy very unripe green mangoes. Wash and cut into very thin slices, dry in the sun, powder and refrigerate.

- Pomegranate seeds can be dried in the sun and stored in an airtight jar.

- When tomatoes are in short supply use mango powder or dried pomegranate seeds as souring agents to give a tang to the dish.

- **To prepare khoya at home:** Cook pure milk over very low heat stirring continuously till all moisture evaporates and it turns dry.

TABLE OF MEASURES

The cup measure used in this book is a 200 ml cup

1 tsp = 5 ml
1 tbsp = 3 tsp
A pinch = $1/8$ tsp (literally a pinch)
A dash = 1-2 drops

All spoon measures are level

Basic Procedures and Recipes

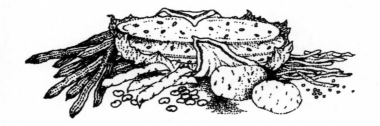

STEAMING

Steaming is one of the healthiest forms of cooking. A steamer consists of two pans that fit firmly on top of each other with a tight-fitting lid. Water is placed in the lower pan and the food to be steamed in the upper one, which has a perforated base through which the steam can rise. The water in the lower pan must always be on the boil and replaced with boiling hot water.

If you don't have a steamer you can improvise one. Take a large pan with a tight fitting lid. Place a bowl in it and pour water into the pan to come half way up the bowl. Bring the water to boil and place the food to be steamed in the bowl. Cover pan and steam the food for the time given in the recipe.

TAMARIND JUICE
Makes: ½ cup

A lime-sized ball of tamarind

- Soak tamarind in ½ cup hot water for 15 minutes.
- Squeeze with your hands to soften tamarind pulp.
- Strain juice and discard pulp.

GHEE
Clarified Butter
Makes: 1½-2 cups

Sindhis are very fond of pure ghee and they use plenty of it in their cooking. There is a saying that 'a dish not covered with a layer of ghee is unfit for a true blue-blooded Sindhi'. In the old days Sindhis only used ghee for cooking. It imparts a flavour to a dish which oil cannot. In this book I have used oil in most recipes except where you cannot achieve the right flavour without ghee.

3-4 cups cream from boiled and cooled milk
1 betel leaf (paan)

- Place cream in a large pan over very low heat. Cook stirring continuously till a brown residue settles at the base of pan and ghee rises to the surface.

- Cool, strain and bottle with a betel leaf, to prevent it from turning rancid.

DHANIA-JEERA MASALA
Coriander-cumin Powder
Makes: 1¾ cups

Use this masala when coriander-cumin powder is called for in the recipes in this book.

1 cup coriander seeds
½ cup cumin seeds
2 tbsp black cumin seeds (kala jeera)

- Roast each ingredient individually on a dry tava or griddle for a few moments till fragrant.
- Cool and grind to a fine powder.
- Store in an airtight jar and use as required.

SINDHI GARAM MASALA POWDER
Makes: 3 cups

Use this masala for the authentic Sindhi taste when garam masala powder is called for in the recipes in this book.

½ cup cloves
½ cup broken cinnamon sticks
8 black cardamoms
½ cup green cardamoms
4 tbsp cumin seeds
½ cup black cumin seeds (kala jeera)
1 nutmeg, grated
1 tsp mace flakes (jaiphal)
10 bay leaves (tej patta)

- Roast each ingredient individually on a dry tava or griddle for a few moments till fragrant.

- Cool and grind to a fine powder.

- Store in an airtight jar and use as required.

Vegetables

SAIYOON PATATAN MEIN
Vermicelli with Potatoes
Serves: 4

Vermicelli:

3 tbsp ghee
2 cups roasted vermicelli (sevian)
3 green cardamoms
½ cup sugar

Potatoes:

5 tbsp ghee
3 medium potatoes, peeled and cut into thick round slices
2 tbsp minced green chillies
2 tbsp finely chopped coriander leaves
¼ tsp turmeric powder
¼ tsp red chilli powder
1 tsp coriander-cumin powder
¼ tsp salt

- Heat ghee for vermicelli in a frying pan over low heat. Add vermicelli and cardamoms and fry stirring continuously for 5 minutes till vermicelli is light brown.

- Stir in sugar and 2 cups water. Cook over low heat stirring occasionally till vermicelli is tender and dry. Remove from heat and set aside.

- Heat ghee for potatoes in a pan over moderate heat. Add remaining ingredients for potatoes, mix well and cover pan. Sprinkle some water on lid and cook over low heat till potatoes are tender.

- Serve hot with vermicelli and a mango pickle for breakfast.

PATATAN MEIN BHINDIYOON
Okra with Potatoes
Serves: 4

250 gms okra (bhindi)
3 tbsp oil
1 large tomato, diced
4 green chillies, slit
2 medium potatoes, boiled, peeled and cut into finger chips

Ground to a fine paste:
2 tbsp chopped coriander leaves
1 tsp ginger paste
1 tsp garlic paste
¼ tsp turmeric powder
¼ tsp red chilli powder
1 tbsp coriander-cumin powder
½ tsp salt

- Wash okra and wipe dry. Trim okra heads and make a slit to come halfway down. Fill ground paste into okra.

- Heat oil in a kadhai or deep frying pan over moderate heat. Add okra and fry for 2-3 minutes.

- Stir in tomato and green chillies and cover pan. Sprinkle some water on lid and cook over low heat for about 5 minutes till okra are almost tender.

- Gently mix in potatoes and cook for a few minutes longer.

- Serve hot with roti.

The Essential Sindhi Cookbook

THOOM MEIN BHINDIYOON
Okra with Garlic
Serves: 2

250 gms okra (bhindi)
2 tbsp oil
1 large tomato, diced

Ground to a fine paste:
1 tsp grated ginger
1 tbsp minced garlic
4 green chillies, chopped
2 tbsp chopped coriander leaves
¼ tsp turmeric powder
¼ tsp red chilli powder
1 tbsp coriander-cumin powder
A large pinch monosodium glutamate (optional)
¼ tsp salt

- Wash okra and wipe dry. Trim okra heads and make a slit to come halfway down. Fill ground paste into okra.

- Heat oil in a kadhai or deep frying pan over moderate heat. Add okra and fry for 2-3 minutes.

- Gently mix in tomato and cover pan. Cook over low heat for about 10 minutes till okra are tender.

- Serve hot with roti.

BHINDIYOON BASAR MEIN
Okra with Onions
Serves: 3

250 gms okra (bhindi)
2 tbsp oil
2 large onions, finely sliced
1 tsp julienned ginger
1 tsp minced garlic
1 large tomato, diced
4 green chillies, cut into 1" slivers
2 tbsp chopped coriander leaves
8 mint leaves, chopped
¼ tsp turmeric powder
¼ tsp red chilli powder
1 tbsp coriander-cumin powder
¼ tsp salt

- Wash okra and pat dry. Top and tail okra and cut into 1" pieces.

- Heat oil in a kadhai or deep frying pan over moderate heat. Add onions, ginger and garlic and fry till onions turn translucent.

- Stir in remaining ingredients and cover pan. Cook over low heat for about 10 minutes till okra are tender.

- Serve hot with roti.

METHI MEIN GUL GOBHI
Cauliflower with Fenugreek Leaves
Serves: 4

4 tbsp oil
1 medium cauliflower (500 gms), cut into florets
1 tsp grated ginger
1 tsp minced garlic
2 cups (100 gms) chopped fenugreek leaves (methi)
3 green chillies, minced
4 tbsp chopped coriander leaves
½ tsp turmeric powder
½ tsp red chilli powder
1 tbsp coriander-cumin powder
½ tsp salt
2 medium tomatoes, diced

- Heat oil in a kadhai or deep frying pan over moderate heat. Add cauliflower and fry till light gold. Drain and set aside.

- Add ginger and garlic to pan and fry for a few moments. Stir in fenugreek leaves, green chillies, coriander leaves, spice powders and salt. Cook stirring occasionally for about 10 minutes till well blended.

- Mix in cauliflower and tomatoes and cover pan. Cook over low heat for about 10 minutes till cauliflower is tender.

- Serve hot with roti.

MASALÉ MEIN GUL GOBHI
Masala Cauliflower
Serves: 4

4 tbsp oil
1 medium cauliflower (500 gms), cut into florets
2 medium tomatoes, finely chopped
4 green chillies, minced
¼ tsp turmeric powder
½ tsp red chilli powder
½ tsp garam masala powder
½ tsp salt

Ground to a paste:
2 medium onions, roughly chopped
1 tsp ginger paste
1 tsp garlic paste

Garnish:
4 tbsp curd, whisked
2 tbsp finely chopped coriander leaves

- Heat oil in a kadhai or deep frying pan over moderate heat. Add cauliflower and fry till light gold. Drain and set aside.

- Add onion paste to pan and fry till light brown. Stir in tomatoes, green chillies, spice powders and salt. Cook stirring occasionally for about 5 minutes till gravy thickens.

- Mix in cauliflower with 1 cup water. Cook for 10 minutes, till cauliflower is tender and almost dry.

- Sprinkle with curd, garnish with coriander leaves and serve hot with roti or rice.

PALAK MEIN GUL GOBHI
Cauliflower with Spinach
Serves: 4

4 tbsp oil
1 medium cauliflower (500 gms), cut into florets
1 tsp ginger paste
1 tsp garlic paste
4 green chillies, minced
2 cups (100 gms) chopped spinach leaves
½ cup (25 gms) chopped fenugreek leaves (methi)
½ cup chopped coriander leaves
8 mint leaves, chopped
½ tsp turmeric powder
½ tsp red chilli powder
1 tbsp coriander-cumin powder
½ tsp salt
1 large tomato, diced

- Heat oil in a kadhai or deep frying pan over moderate heat. Add cauliflower and fry till light gold. Drain and set aside.

- Add ginger and garlic to pan and stir-fry over low heat for about 1 minute. Stir in green chillies, spinach, fenugreek, coriander and mint leaves, spice powders and salt. Cook for about 10 minutes till well blended.

- Mix in cauliflower and tomato. Cook over low heat for about 10 minutes till cauliflower is tender and gravy thickens.

- Serve hot with roti.

MASALÉWARA VANGAN
Spicy Aubergines
Serves: 4

1 large purple aubergine (baingan), cut into thick rounds
¼ tsp + ¼ tsp salt
Oil for deep frying
½ tsp cumin seeds
1 medium onion, minced
1 tsp ginger paste
1 tsp garlic paste
2 green chillies, minced
¼ tsp turmeric powder
¼ tsp red chilli powder
1 tsp coriander-cumin powder
1 large tomato, finely chopped
6 tbsp crumbled cottage cheese (paneer)

Garnish:
2 tbsp chopped coriander leaves

- Rub ¼ tsp salt into aubergine slices and set aside to marinate for about 30 minutes.

- Heat 2 tbsp oil in a pan over moderate heat and add cumin seeds. When they stop spluttering, add onion, ginger, garlic and green chillies. Fry till onion turns translucent.

- Stir in ¼ tsp salt, spice powders and tomato. Cook for about 5 minutes till gravy thickens.

- Mix in paneer and cook for a few minutes longer. Remove from heat and set aside.

- Heat oil for deep frying in a kadhai or deep frying pan

over moderate heat. Squeeze out water from aubergine slices and fry till golden on both sides. Drain and place on kitchen paper to absorb excess oil.

- Arrange aubergine slices on a platter, spread some spiced paneer on each slice, garnish with coriander leaves and serve with roti or parathé.

TARIYAL VANGAN
Fried Aubergines
Serves: 4

1 large purple aubergine (baingan), cut into thick rounds
½ tsp salt
Oil for deep frying

Mixed together:

1 tsp red chilli powder
1 tbsp coriander-cumin powder
1 tbsp mango powder (amchur)

Mixed together for garnish:

1 medium tomato, finely chopped
½ tsp julienned ginger
2 green chillies, minced
2 tbsp finely chopped coriander leaves

- Rub salt into aubergine slices and set aside to marinate for about 30 minutes.

- Heat oil in a kadhai or deep frying pan over moderate heat. Squeeze out water from aubergine slices and fry till golden on both sides. Drain and place on kitchen paper to absorb excess oil.

- Arrange aubergine slices on a flat platter and sprinkle with mixed spices and garnish.

- Serve with roti or dal and rice.

BHARIYAL KARELA
Stuffed Bittergourds
Serves: 4

6 medium bittergourds (karela)
¼ tsp salt
4 tbsp oil

Filling:

1 cup (50 gms) fenugreek leaves (methi)
1 small onion, roughly chopped
1 tsp ginger paste
1 tsp garlic paste
4 green chillies, roughly chopped
3 tbsp chopped coriander leaves
3 tbsp thick tamarind juice
½ tsp turmeric powder
½ tsp red chilli powder
1 tbsp coriander-cumin powder
¼ tsp salt

- Peel bittergourds and make a slit in the centre to come halfway down. Rub in salt and set aside for about 24 hours. Rinse thoroughly and squeeze out water.

- Scoop out seeds from bittergourds and grind to a coarse paste with all ingredients for filling.

- Stuff bittergourds with filling and tie with cotton thread.

- Heat oil in a large frying pan and place bittergourds in a single layer in pan. Fry turning occasionally till golden on all sides. Drain and remove from pan.

- Remove thread and serve hot with roti or parathé.

KHATTA MITHA KARELA
Sweet and Sour Bittergourds
Serves: 4

6 medium bittergourds (karela)
½ tsp salt
1 tbsp + 3 tbsp oil
2 tbsp grated jaggery
4 tbsp thick tamarind juice

Filling:

2 medium onions, roughly chopped
1 tsp minced ginger
1 tsp minced garlic
¼ cup coriander leaves, chopped
¼ cup mint leaves, chopped
½ tsp turmeric powder
½ tsp red chilli powder
1 tbsp coriander-cumin powder
½ tsp salt

- Peel bittergourds and make a slit in the centre to come halfway down. Rub in salt and set aside for about 24 hours. Rinse thoroughly and squeeze out water.

- Scoop out seeds from bittergourds and grind to a coarse paste with all ingredients for filling.

- Heat 1 tbsp oil in a frying pan over moderate heat and add ground paste. Fry stirring continuously for about 5 minutes till oil rises to the surface. Remove from heat and mix in jaggery and tamarind.

- Stuff bittergourds with filling and tie with cotton thread.

The Essential Sindhi Cookbook

- Heat 3 tbsp oil in a large frying pan and place bittergourds in a single layer in pan. Fry turning occasionally till golden on all sides. Drain and remove from pan.

- Remove thread and serve hot with roti or parathé.

KOOT PATATA
Crisp-fried Potatoes
Serves: 3

4 medium potatoes
Oil for deep frying
½ tsp pepper powder
½ tsp red chilli powder
1 tbsp coriander-cumin powder
1 tbsp mango powder (amchur)
¾ tsp salt

- Peel potatoes, wash and cut into ½" thick round slices.

- Heat oil in a kadhai or deep frying pan and fry potatoes till just starting to change colour. Drain and place on kitchen paper till completely cooled. Press each slice between your palms to flatten them.

- Heat oil again and fry potatoes till crisp and golden. Drain and place on kitchen paper to absorb excess oil.

- Mix together spice powders and salt and sprinkle over potatoes.

- Serve hot with Sindhi curry (p. 64) and rice.

KARELA PATATAN MEIN
Bittergourds with Potatoes
Serves: 5

6 medium bittergourds (karela)
½ tsp + ¼ tsp salt
½ tsp turmeric powder
½ tsp red chilli powder
1 tbsp coriander-cumin powder
4 tbsp oil
1 large potato, peeled and cubed
2 large onions, finely sliced
2 medium tomatoes, diced

Ground to a paste:
1 tsp grated ginger
1 tsp minced garlic
4 green chillies, roughly chopped
½ cup chopped coriander leaves
6 mint leaves, chopped

- Peel bittergourds and make a slit in the centre to come halfway down. Rub in ½ tsp salt and set aside for about 24 hours. Rinse and squeeze out water.

- Mix together ¼ tsp salt, spice powders and ground paste and fill into bittergourds.

- Heat oil in a kadhai or deep frying pan over moderate heat, add potato and fry till tender and golden. Drain and set aside.

- Add bittergourds to pan and fry till golden. Drain and set aside.

- Add onions to pan and fry till translucent. Mix in

bittergourds, potato and tomatoes. Cook over low heat for about 5 minutes till tomatoes are soft and gravy thickens.

- Serve hot with roti.

MASALÉWARA BHIEN
Spicy Lotus Stems
Serves: 3

250 gms lotus stems (kamal kakdi)
3 tbsp oil
1 cup (50 gms) chopped spinach leaves
1 cup (50 gms) chopped fenugreek leaves (methi)
¼ cup chopped green garlic or 1 tsp chopped garlic
4 green chillies, minced
¼ tsp turmeric powder
¼ tsp red chilli powder
1 tbsp coriander-cumin powder
1 tbsp mango powder (amchur)
½ tsp salt
1 medium tomato, diced

- Prepare and boil lotus stems as given on p. 29.

- Heat oil in a pan over moderate heat. Add spinach, fenugreek leaves, garlic, green chillies, spice powders and salt. Cook stirring occasionally for 5-7 minutes till well blended.

- Mix in lotus stems and tomato. Cook over low heat for about 3 minutes till tomato is soft and gravy thickens.

- Serve with roti.

BHIEN PATATAN MEIN
Lotus Stems with Potatoes
Serves: 4

250 gms lotus stems (kamal kakdi)
2 tbsp oil
12-15 cloves garlic, chopped
2 medium tomatoes, blanched, peeled and puréed
¼ tsp turmeric powder
¼ tsp red chilli powder
2 medium potatoes, peeled and cubed
4 green chillies, slit
2 tbsp chopped coriander leaves
½ tsp salt

Tempering:

1 tbsp oil
1 tsp mustard seeds
2 dry red chillies, broken

- Prepare and boil lotus stems as given on p. 29.

- Heat oil in a pan over moderate heat. Add garlic and fry lightly for a few moments. Mix in tomatoes and spice powders. Cook for about 5 minutes till gravy thickens. Add remaining ingredients except tempering. Stir in 1 cup water and cook for 5-7 minutes till potatoes are tender.

- Heat oil for tempering in a small pan over moderate heat and add mustard seeds and red chillies. When mustard seeds stop spluttering, pour contents of pan over vegetables.

- Serve hot with roti.

BHIEN JO KHEEMO
Minced Lotus Stems
Serves: 4

250 gms lotus stems (kamal kakdi)
3 tbsp oil
1 medium onion, minced
1 tsp ginger paste
1 tsp garlic paste
4 green chillies, minced
2 medium tomatoes, chopped
2 tbsp curd, whisked
¼ tsp turmeric powder
½ tsp red chilli powder
1 tbsp coriander-cumin powder
¼ tsp garam masala powder
½ tsp salt
1 cup shelled green peas, boiled

Garnish:

2 tbsp chopped coriander leaves

- Prepare lotus stems as given on p. 29. Do not boil them. Grind lotus stems coarsely.

- Heat oil in a frying pan over moderate heat. Add lotus stems and fry till golden. Drain and set aside.

- Add onion, ginger and garlic to pan and fry till onion turns translucent. Mix in green chillies, tomatoes, curd, spice powders and salt. Stir in lotus stems and cook over low heat for about 5 minutes till gravy thickens.

- Mix in green peas and cook for a few minutes longer.

- Garnish with coriander leaves and serve hot with roti or rice.

KACHALUN JI BHAAJI
Spicy Colocasia
Serves: 2

250 gms colocasia (arbi)
3 tbsp oil
1 medium onion, minced
1 tsp minced ginger
1 tsp minced garlic
2 green chillies, minced
4 curry leaves
½ tsp cumin seeds
¼ tsp turmeric powder
¼ tsp red chilli powder
1 tsp coriander-cumin powder
½ tsp salt
2 medium tomatoes, blanched, peeled and puréed

Garnish:
2 tbsp chopped coriander leaves

- Peel colocasia, wash well and cut lengthwise into 4 pieces each.

- Heat oil in a kadhai or deep frying pan over moderate heat. Add colocasia and fry till golden. Drain and set aside.

- Add onion, ginger, garlic, green chillies and curry leaves to pan and fry till onion turns translucent.

- Stir in colocasia, cumin seeds, spice powders, salt and tomatoes. Cook over low heat for about 5 minutes till gravy thickens.

- Garnish with coriander leaves and serve hot with roti.

TARIYAL KACHALU
Fried Colocasia
Serves: 3

250 gms colocasia (arbi)
¼ cup semolina (rava/sooji)
2 tbsp sesame seeds (til)
¼ tsp salt
5 tbsp oil

Filling:

½ tsp red chilli powder
1 tsp coriander-cumin powder
¼ tsp garam masala powder
½ tsp mango powder (amchur)

- Wash colocasia and boil in enough water to cover for about 15 minutes till nearly tender. Cool, peel and make a slit in the centre of each colocasia to come halfway down.

- Mix together all ingredients for filling and stuff into colocasia. Gently press each colocasia between your palms to flatten slightly.

- Mix together semolina, sesame seeds and salt. Roll each colocasia in mixture to coat completely.

- Heat oil in a large frying pan over moderate heat and fry colocasia in batches till light brown. Drain and place on kitchen paper to absorb excess oil.

- Serve hot with plain dal and rice.

SAI BHAAJI
Sindhi Spinach
Serves: 6

4 tbsp oil
1 large onion, minced
1 tsp ginger paste
1 tsp garlic paste
4 green chillies, minced
2 cups (100 gms) chopped spinach leaves
½ cup (25 gms) chopped fenugreek leaves (methi)
¼ cup chopped coriander leaves
2 cups mixed chopped vegetables—red pumpkin (kaddu), potatoes,
carrots, and aubergine (baingan)
4 medium tomatoes, diced
½ cup husked Bengal gram (chana dal)
½ tsp turmeric powder
½ tsp red chilli powder
1 tbsp coriander-cumin powder
1 tsp salt

Tempering:

1 tbsp oil
1 tsp cumin seeds
A large pinch asafoetida powder (hing)

- Heat oil in a kadhai or deep frying pan over moderate heat. Add onion, ginger, garlic and green chillies and fry till onion turns translucent.

- Add remaining ingredients except tempering with 1 cup water. Cook over moderate heat for about 15 minutes till vegetables are soft and mushy. Remove from heat and cool.

- Place vegetables in a blender and blend for 2 seconds

only. Return to pan and heat through.

- Heat oil for tempering in a small pan over moderate heat and add cumin seeds and asafoetida. When cumin seeds stop spluttering, pour contents of pan over vegetables.

- Serve hot with khichdi (p. 143).

SEYAL KOFTA
Vegetable Kofta in an Onion Curry
Serves: 4

Kofté:

½ cup husked Bengal gram (chana dal)
2 tbsp oil
1 medium onion, minced
1 tsp ginger-garlic paste
2 cups (100 gms) chopped spinach leaves
¼ cup chopped coriander leaves
1 medium tomato, chopped
¼ tsp red chilli powder
1 tsp coriander-cumin powder
¾ tsp salt
½ cup gram flour (besan)
Oil for deep frying

Curry:

1 tbsp oil
1 tsp cumin seeds
2 large onions, minced
1 tsp minced ginger
1 tsp minced garlic
4 green chillies, minced
3 tbsp chopped coriander leaves
2 medium tomatoes, diced
¼ tsp turmeric powder
¼ tsp red chilli powder
1 tbsp coriander-cumin powder
½ tsp salt

- Wash dal and soak in water for 30 minutes.

- Heat 2 tbsp oil for kofté in a pan over moderate heat. Add onion and ginger-garlic paste and fry till onion turns translucent.

The Essential Sindhi Cookbook

- Drain dal and add to pan with remaining ingredients for kofté except gram flour and oil for deep frying. Mix well and stir in 1 cup water. Cook for about 30 minutes till dal and vegetables are tender and dry.

- Remove from heat and cool. Knead till well blended.

- Mix in gram flour and shape into marble-sized balls.

- Heat oil for deep frying in a kadhai or deep frying pan and fry kofté in batches till golden. Drain and place on kitchen paper to absorb excess oil.

- Heat oil for curry in a pan over moderate heat. Add cumin seeds and when they stop spluttering, add onions, ginger and garlic and fry till onions turn translucent.

- Stir in remaining ingredients for curry and cook for about 5 minutes till well blended.

- Gently mix in kofté and serve with roti.

KARI PALAK
Black Spinach
Serves: 4

This is a very famous dish from Sindh. It is made in an iron pan and it looks black in colour. It is full of the goodness of iron because spinach is rich in iron and the pan in which it is cooked is supposed to impart iron to the food.

2 tbsp ghee or oil
2 cups (100 gms) chopped spinach leaves
1 medium purple aubergine (baingan), chopped
1 large tomato, diced
4 green chillies, minced
1 tsp ginger-garlic paste
½ tsp red chilli powder
1 tbsp coriander-cumin powder
½ tsp salt
1 tbsp hot ghee

- Heat 2 tbsp ghee or oil over low heat in a black iron kadhai (if possible). Add remaining ingredients except 1 tbsp ghee and mix well. Cook for about 15 minutes till vegetables are tender.

- Remove from heat and mash to a paste with a wooden spoon. Return pan to moderate heat and heat through.

- Pour 1 tbsp hot ghee over vegetables and serve hot with roti.

SAI BHAAJI PATATAN MEIN
Spinach with Potatoes
Serves: 4

3 tbsp oil
2 large potatoes, peeled and cubed
1 medium onion, minced
½ tsp grated ginger
½ tsp minced garlic
2 cups (100 gms) chopped spinach leaves
1 medium tomato, diced
1 tbsp coriander-cumin powder
¼ tsp turmeric powder
¼ tsp red chilli powder
½ tsp salt

Tempering:

1 tbsp oil
1 tsp cumin seeds

- Heat oil in a kadhai or deep frying pan over moderate heat. Add potatoes and fry till golden. Drain and set aside.

- Add onion, ginger and garlic to pan and fry till onion turns translucent.

- Mix in potatoes with remaining ingredients except tempering. Cook over low heat stirring occasionally for about 10 minutes till vegetables are tender.

- Heat oil for tempering in a small pan over moderate heat and add cumin seeds. When they stop spluttering, pour contents of pan over vegetables.

- Serve hot with roti or rice.

SINDHI CURRY
Serves: 4

This dish is served at marriages and all other special occasions, when vegetarian food is served. Two to three tablespoons of rice are placed in a soup bowl and the bowl is filled with curry. Koot patata are served as a side dish and boondi ladoo are generally broken and sprinkled over the curry.

250 gms lotus stems (kamal kakdi)
2 medium potatoes
250 gms mixed vegetables—capsicums, small aubergines (baingan), carrots and French beans
2 tbsp + 4 tbsp oil
1 cup gram flour (besan)
½ cup chopped tomatoes
1 tsp minced ginger
4 thick green chillies, slit
2 tbsp chopped coriander leaves
8 curry leaves
1 tsp turmeric powder
1½ tsp salt
½ cup thick tamarind juice

Tempering:

2 tbsp oil
½ tsp mustard seeds
½ tsp fenugreek seeds (methi)
½ tsp cumin seeds
¼ tsp asafoetida powder (hing)

- Prepare and boil lotus stems as given on p. 29.
- Parboil potatoes, peel and cut into quarters.

- Remove pith and seeds of capsicums and cut into quarters.

- Cut aubergines into quarters.

- Scrape carrots and cut into ½" rounds.

- Trim and string French beans and cut into 2" pieces.

- Heat 2 tbsp oil in a pan over moderate heat. Add vegetables and stir-fry for 2-3 minutes. Remove from heat and set aside.

- Heat 4 tbsp oil in a large pan over low heat. Add gram flour and fry stirring continuously till red. Remove pan from heat and slowly pour in 5 cups water, stirring vigorously to blend.

- Return pan to low heat and mix in remaining ingredients except tempering. Cover pan and simmer for 15-20 minutes stirring occasionally, till vegetables are tender.

- Heat oil for tempering in a small pan over moderate heat and add remaining ingredients for tempering. When mustard seeds stop spluttering, pour contents of pan over curry.

- Serve hot with rice, koot patata (p. 51) and boondi ladoo.

TAMATAN JI CURRY
Tomato Curry
Serves: 6

250 gms okra (bhindi)
250 gms mixed vegetables—potatoes, aubergines (baingan) and
cauliflower
1 tbsp oil
2 tbsp gram flour (besan)
1 tsp minced ginger
6 large tomatoes, blanched, peeled and puréed
2 tbsp chopped coriander leaves
8 curry leaves
1 tsp turmeric powder
1½ tsp salt

Tempering:

3 tbsp oil
½ tsp mustard seeds
½ tsp fenugreek seeds (methi)
½ tsp cumin seeds
¼ tsp asafoetida powder (hing)

Garnish:

2 tbsp chopped coriander leaves

- Wash okra and wipe dry. Trim okra heads and make a slit to come halfway down.

- Peel and cut potatoes into 1" cubes.

- Cut aubergines into 1" cubes.

- Cut cauliflower into small florets.

- Heat oil in a large frying pan over moderate heat. Add vegetables, one at a time and stir-fry individually for

2-3 minutes each. Drain and set each vegetable aside separately.

- Mix gram flour with 2 cups water. Whisk well and set aside.

- Heat oil for tempering in a large pan over moderate heat and add remaining ingredients for tempering. When mustard seeds stop spluttering, add remaining ingredients except okra, aubergines and garnish. Mix well and simmer over low heat for about 10 minutes till vegetables are half cooked.

- Add okra and aubergines and continue to cook for another 10 minutes till vegetables are tender.

- Garnish with coriander leaves and serve hot with rice.

SURAN JO KHEEMO
Minced Yam
Serves: 4

3 tbsp oil
1 tsp cumin seeds
1 medium onion, minced
1 tsp minced ginger
½ tsp minced garlic
2 green chillies, minced
250 gms yam (zimikand), peeled and grated
1 large tomato, finely chopped
2 tbsp chopped coriander leaves
½ tsp turmeric powder
½ tsp red chilli powder
1 tbsp coriander-cumin powder
½ tsp salt

- Heat oil in a kadhai or deep frying pan over moderate heat. Add cumin seeds and when they stop spluttering, add onion, ginger, garlic and green chillies and fry till onion turns translucent.

- Mix in yam and fry stirring occasionally for 6-7 minutes till oil rises to the surface.

- Add remaining ingredients and cook over low heat for about 10 minutes till yam is tender.

- Serve hot with roti.

Seafood

MACHHI JA PAKODA
Fish Fritters
Serves: 4

500 gms pomfret, cleaned and sliced through the bone
1 small onion, minced
1 tsp minced ginger
4 green chillies, minced
1 small tomato, finely chopped
2 tbsp chopped fenugreek leaves (methi)
2 tbsp chopped coriander leaves
4 mint leaves, chopped
1 cup gram flour (besan)
¼ tsp turmeric powder
1 tsp coarsely ground cumin seeds
A pinch sodium bicarbonate
½ tsp salt
Oil for deep frying

- Wash fish and drain. Place in a pan with water to cover and boil for about 10 minutes till tender. Drain. Remove skin and bones and discard. Mash flesh.

- Mix together all ingredients except oil. Add about ½ cup water, a little at a time, and mix to make a thick batter of dropping consistency.

- Heat oil in a kadhai to smoking point over high heat. Lower heat to moderate and drop in teaspoons of batter. Fry pakodé in batches till golden. Drain and place on kitchen paper to absorb excess oil.

- Serve with any chutney of your choice.

Variation: Use steamed, chopped prawns in place of fish.

MACHHI JOON CHAPIYOON
Fish Cutlets
Serves: 4

500 gms pomfret, cleaned and sliced through the bone
1 medium potato, boiled, peeled and mashed
2 bread slices soaked in water and squeezed dry
1 tsp cumin seeds
½ tsp salt
1 cup fine breadcrumbs or powdered cornflakes
Oil for shallow frying

Filling:

1 large onion, minced
4 green chillies, minced
1 tsp minced ginger
2 tbsp chopped coriander leaves
8 mint leaves, chopped
¼ tsp turmeric powder
¼ tsp red chilli powder
½ tsp coriander-cumin powder
½ tsp garam masala powder
¼ tsp salt

- Wash fish and drain. Place in a pan with water to cover and boil for about 10 minutes till tender. Drain. Remove skin and bones and discard. Mash flesh.

- Mix fish, potato, bread, cumin seeds and salt in a bowl and knead to a smooth paste.

- Combine ingredients for filling and mix well.

- Divide fish paste and filling into equal portions and shape into balls. Flatten fish balls, place filling in the centre and work fish paste around to cover filling completely. Reshape into balls and flatten to form round cutlets. Coat with breadcrumbs or cornflakes and set aside.

- Heat oil in a frying pan over moderate heat and fry cutlets in batches till brown on both sides. Drain and place on kitchen paper to absorb excess oil.

- Serve hot with any chutney of your choice.

METHI MEIN MACHHI
Fish with Fenugreek Leaves
Serves: 6

1 kg pomfret, cleaned and sliced through the bone
4 tbsp oil
4 tbsp cornflour
1 tbsp ginger paste
1 tbsp garlic paste
3 cups (150 gms) chopped fenugreek leaves (methi)
½ cup chopped coriander leaves
10 mint leaves, chopped
1 tsp red chilli powder
1 tbsp coriander-cumin powder
½ tsp salt
3 large tomatoes, chopped

Marinade:

1 tsp turmeric powder
½ tsp salt
Juice of 1 lime

- Wash fish and pat dry.

- Combine ingredients for marinade, rub into fish and marinate for 1 hour. Rinse well and drain thoroughly.

- Heat oil in a frying pan over moderate heat. Coat fish lightly with cornflour and fry in batches till light brown on both sides. Drain and place on kitchen paper to absorb excess oil.

- Add ginger and garlic to pan and fry for a few moments. Mix in fenugreek, coriander and mint leaves, spice powders and salt. Cook over low heat for 2-3 minutes till well blended.

The Essential Sindhi Cookbook

- Stir in tomatoes and cook for about 10 minutes till well blended.

- Add fish and mix gently. Cover pan and cook over low heat for 2-3 minutes longer.

- Serve hot with rice.

TAMATAN MEIN MACHHI
Tomato Fish
Serves: 4

500 gms pomfret, cleaned and sliced through the bone
4 tbsp oil
2 tbsp cornflour
6 large tomatoes, chopped
4 green chillies, minced
4 tbsp chopped coriander leaves
10 mint leaves, chopped
1 tsp grated ginger
¼ cup chopped green garlic or 1 tsp chopped garlic
1 tbsp coriander-cumin powder
½ tsp garam masala powder
½ tsp salt

Marinade:

½ tsp turmeric powder
½ tsp salt
1 tbsp lime juice

Tempering:

1 tsp oil
1 tsp cumin seeds

- Wash fish and pat dry.

- Combine ingredients for marinade, rub into fish and marinate for 1 hour. Rinse well and drain thoroughly.

- Heat oil in a frying pan over moderate heat. Coat fish lightly with cornflour and fry in batches till light brown on both sides. Drain and place on kitchen paper to absorb excess oil.

- Add remaining ingredients except tempering to pan. Cook for about 10 minutes stirring occasionally till well blended.

- Gently mix in fish and cover pan. Cook over low heat for 2-3 minutes longer.

- Heat oil for tempering in a small pan over moderate heat and add cumin seeds. When they stop spluttering, pour contents of pan over fish.

- Serve hot with roti.

GOGRUN MEIN MACHHI
Fish with Turnips
Serves: 4

500 gms pomfret, cleaned and sliced through the bone
4 tbsp oil
6 cloves garlic, crushed
250 gms turnips, peeled and cut into quarters
½ tsp red chilli powder
1 tbsp coriander-cumin powder
½ tsp salt
½ tsp plain flour (maida) mixed with 2 tbsp water
4 green chillies, minced
2 tbsp chopped coriander leaves

Marinade:

½ tsp turmeric powder
½ tsp salt
1 tbsp lime juice

Tempering:

1 tsp oil
1 tsp mustard seeds

- Wash fish and pat dry.

- Combine ingredients for marinade, rub into fish and marinate for 1 hour. Rinse well and drain thoroughly.

- Heat oil in a frying pan over moderate heat. Add fish and fry lightly on both sides. Drain and place on kitchen paper to absorb excess oil.

- Add garlic to pan and fry for a few moments.

- Mix in fish, turnips, spice powders, salt and 2 cups water. Cook over low heat for about 10 minutes stirring occasionally till fish is tender.

- Gently blend in flour paste, green chillies and coriander leaves. Cook stirring occasionally till gravy thickens.

- Heat oil for tempering in a small pan over moderate heat and add mustard seeds. When they stop spluttering, pour contents of pan over fish.

- Serve hot with roti.

PALO KOK
Baked Fish
Serves: 4

This is a famous and delightfully delicious fish dish from Sindh. It is generally served as a snack with drinks. Once the fish has been eaten, the masala is scooped up with phulko.

2 x 500 gms fish (palo/hilsa), kept whole
½ tsp turmeric powder
3 tsp red chilli powder
6 tbsp thick tamarind juice
4 tbsp rum (optional)
8 tbsp oil

Marinade:

1 tsp turmeric powder
1 tbsp salt
2 tbsp white vinegar

Ground to a paste:
4 large onions, roughly chopped
1 tbsp ginger paste
1 tbsp garlic paste
6 green chillies, chopped
4 tbsp chopped coriander leaves

- Clean, scale and gut fish. Cut into half lengthwise, along the backbone. Wash well and pat dry.

- Combine ingredients for marinade, rub into fish and marinate for 1 hour. Rinse well and drain thoroughly.

- Mix onion paste with spice powders, tamarind and

rum (if used) and set aside.

- Heat oil in a large frying pan over moderate heat. Place fish in pan in a single layer with the cut side down. Fry till the underside turns brown. Turn over, spread spice paste in a thick layer over fish and fry for 5 minutes longer.

- Transfer fish carefully to a greased baking tray. Bake in an oven preheated to 180°C (350°F) for 15 minutes. Turn fish over and bake for 15 minutes longer.

- Serve hot.

DHAKIYAL MACHHI
Baked Fish
Serves: 4

This fish was originally cooked in sand on the river beds or seashore and was called wadi ji macchi. It is served with an accompaniment of green chutney and slices of onions and lime. It is a delicious fish dish.

2 x 500 gms fish (palo/hilsa), kept whole
1½ cups plain flour (maida)
1 cup thick tamarind juice
8 tbsp ghee

Ground to a paste:

2 large onions, roughly chopped
1 tbsp grated ginger
1 tbsp minced garlic
4 green chillies, chopped
1 cup chopped coriander leaves
¼ cup chopped mint leaves
2 tbsp red chilli powder
1 tbsp coriander-cumin powder

Marinade:

1 tsp turmeric powder
1 tbsp salt
Juice of 1 lime

- Clean, scale and gut fish. Make fine gashes with a knife on both sides of fish without separating the pieces. Wash well and pat dry.

- Combine ingredients for marinade, rub into fish and marinate for 1 hour. Rinse well and drain thoroughly.

82   *The Essential Sindhi Cookbook*

- Make a stiff dough with flour and ½ cup water and set aside.

- Mix spice paste with tamarind juice and ghee. Fill fish cavities with paste and rub remaining paste all over fish.

- Divide dough into 4 portions and roll out each portion into a thick roti, large enough to hold a fish.

- Place a fish in the centre of 2 roti. Moisten edges of all roti and cover fish with the other 2 roti. Press edges of roti firmly with your fingers to seal.

- Carefully transfer fish to a greased baking tray. Bake in an oven preheated to 180°C (350°F) for 30 minutes till crust is golden.

- Break open crust and serve fish immediately with sai chutney (p. 226) and slices of onions and lime.

Note: You can cook the fish in sand in your own home. Fill a deep pan with sand and heat it thoroughly. Bury the fish wrapped in dough in the hot sand and remove after 1 hour.

MACHHI JA MASALÉWARA PAKODA
Spicy Batter-fried Fish
Serves: 4

500 gms pomfret fillets, cut into 2" squares
Oil for deep frying

Batter:

½ cup gram flour (besan)
¼ tsp salt
¼ tsp red chilli powder
¼ tsp cumin seeds
A pinch sodium bicarbonate
A pinch monosodium glutamate (optional)
1 tbsp chopped coriander leaves (optional)
1 green chilli, minced

- Wash fish fillets. Steam for about 5 minutes till almost tender.

- Combine all ingredients for batter. Add about ¼ cup water, a little at a time, and mix to make a thick, smooth batter.

- Heat oil in a kadhai or deep frying pan to smoking point over high heat. Dip fish fillets in batter, lower heat to moderate and fry pakodé in batches till golden. Drain and place on kitchen paper to absorb excess oil.

- Serve with any chutney of your choice.

The Essential Sindhi Cookbook

THOOM MEIN JHINGA
Garlic Prawns
Serves: 4

500 gms prawns, shelled, deveined and cleaned
4 tbsp oil
1 tsp ginger paste
1 tsp garlic paste
1 large tomato, chopped
1 tbsp coriander-cumin powder
½ tsp turmeric powder
2 tbsp chopped coriander leaves
½ tsp red chilli powder
½ tsp salt

- Wash prawns and drain thoroughly.

- Heat oil in a frying pan over moderate heat. Add ginger and garlic and fry for a few moments.

- Mix in remaining ingredients. Cook over low heat for about 10 minutes stirring occasionally till prawns are tender and gravy thickens.

- Serve hot with roti.

DAG MEIN JHINGA
Onion-flavoured Prawn Curry
Serves: 4

500 gms prawns, shelled, deveined and cleaned
4 tbsp oil
1 tsp cumin seeds
2 large onions, minced
1 tsp ginger paste
1 tsp garlic paste
4 green chillies, minced
½ tsp red chilli powder
1 tbsp coriander-cumin powder
½ tsp garam masala powder
½ tsp salt
2 medium tomatoes, chopped
2 tbsp coriander leaves
8 mint leaves, chopped

- Wash prawns and drain thoroughly.

- Heat oil in a pan over moderate heat and add cumin seeds. When they stop spluttering, add onions, ginger, garlic and green chillies and fry till onions turn brown.

- Stir in prawns, spice powders and salt. Cook over low heat for about 10 minutes till water from prawns has evaporated.

- Mix in remaining ingredients and cook till tomatoes are well blended. Stir in 1 cup water and cook for 5 minutes longer.

- Serve hot with rice.

The Essential Sindhi Cookbook

DAHI MEIN JHINGA
Prawns in a Curd-based Curry
Serves: 4

500 gms prawns, shelled, deveined and cleaned
4 tbsp oil
1 medium onion, minced
½ tsp turmeric powder
½ tsp red chilli powder
1 tbsp coriander-cumin powder
½ tsp garam masala powder
¾ tsp salt
1 cup curd, whisked

Ground to a paste:

1 tsp minced ginger
1 tsp minced garlic
4 green chillies, roughly chopped
1 tsp cumin seeds

Garnish:

2 tbsp chopped coriander leaves

- Wash prawns and drain thoroughly.

- Heat oil in a pan over moderate heat. Add onion and fry till translucent. Add prawns and fry for about 5 minutes till water from prawns has evaporated.

- Mix in remaining ingredients except garnish. Cook stirring occasionally till prawns are tender and coated with curry.

- Garnish with coriander leaves and serve hot with roti.

JHINGAN JI CURRY
Prawn Curry
Serves: 4

Kofté:

500 gms prawns, shelled, deveined and cleaned
1 small onion, roughly chopped
1 tsp minced ginger
1 tsp minced garlic
1 egg, whisked
2 tbsp chopped coriander leaves
½ tsp red chilli powder
½ tsp garam masala powder
½ tsp salt
1 cup fine breadcrumbs or powdered cornflakes
Oil for deep frying

Curry:

3 tbsp oil
2 medium onions, minced
½ tsp ginger paste
½ tsp garlic paste
2 medium tomatoes, puréed
1 cup curd, whisked
4 green chillies, slit
2 tbsp chopped coriander leaves
¼ tsp turmeric powder
½ tsp red chilli powder
1 tbsp coriander-cumin powder
1 tsp garam masala powder
½ tsp salt

- Wash prawns and drain thoroughly.

- Grind prawns with remaining ingredients for kofté, except breadcrumbs or cornflakes and oil.

- Shape into marble-sized balls and roll in breadcrumbs or cornflakes to coat completely.

- Heat oil in a kadhai or deep frying pan over moderate heat and fry kofté in batches till brown. Drain and place on kitchen paper to absorb excess oil.

- Heat oil for curry in a pan over moderate heat. Add onions, ginger and garlic and fry till onions turn translucent.

- Blend in tomatoes and curd. Cook over low heat stirring continuously for about 5 minutes till thick.

- Mix in remaining ingredients for curry with 1 cup water and simmer, stirring continuously for 3-4 minutes.

- Place kofté in a serving dish and pour curry over them. Serve hot with rice.

JHINGA PATATAN MEIN
Prawns with Potatoes
Serves: 4

500 gms prawns, shelled, deveined and cleaned
4 tbsp oil
4 green chillies, slit
½ tsp turmeric powder
½ tsp red chilli powder
1 tbsp coriander-cumin powder
½ tsp garam masala powder
½ tsp salt
2 medium potatoes, boiled, peeled and cubed
4 tbsp chopped coriander leaves

- Wash prawns and drain thoroughly.

- Heat oil in a frying pan over low heat. Add prawns and fry for about 5 minutes till water from prawns has evaporated and they turn brown.

- Stir in green chillies, spice powders and salt with 2 cups water and cook for about 5 minutes.

- Add potatoes and coriander leaves and continue simmering till prawns are tender and gravy thickens.

- Serve with rice.

Mutton

MASALÉ MINEN CHAPIYOON
Spicy Mutton Chops
Serves: 4

500 gms mutton chops
4 tbsp ghee or oil

Ground to a paste:

2" piece ginger, chopped
4 green chillies, chopped
4 tbsp chopped coriander leaves
½ tsp red chilli powder
½ tsp black pepper powder
1 tbsp coriander powder
1 tbsp garam masala powder
½ tsp salt

- Wash chops and pat dry. Trim and beat with a wooden mallet to break fibres. Rub spice paste over chops and marinate for 30 minutes.

- Place chops in a frying pan and pour in 1 cup water. Cook over low heat for about 30 minutes till tender and dry.

- Add ghee to pan, raise heat to moderate and fry till chops are brown, turning occasionally.

- Serve with mixed boiled vegetables.

PALAK MEIN TEEVAN
Meat with Spinach
Serves: 4

This dish is always cooked in an iron pan. If you don't have one, use any other pan.

500 gms mutton, with bone
4 tbsp ghee or oil
2 medium onions, minced
1 tsp ginger paste
1 tsp garlic paste
4 green chillies, minced
3 cups (150 gms) chopped spinach leaves
2 medium tomatoes, diced
½ tsp turmeric powder
½ tsp red chilli powder
1 tbsp coriander-cumin powder
½ tsp salt

Garnish:

1 tsp powdered green cardamom
½ cup cream (optional)

- Wash meat, pat dry and cut into serving portions.

- Heat ghee or oil in an iron kadhai (if possible) over moderate heat. Add onions and fry till golden brown.

- Mix in 1 cup water, raise heat to high and bring to boil. Lower heat and add meat, ginger, garlic and green chillies. Cover pan and simmer for about 30 minutes till meat is almost cooked.

- Stir in remaining ingredients except garnish. Cook over low heat for about 40 minutes till meat is tender.

- Place in a serving dish and pour cream (if used) over meat and spinach. Sprinkle cardamom powder on top and serve hot with jowar jo dhodho (p. 182).

PHOTIAN MEIN TEEVAN
Cardamom-flavoured Mutton Curry
Serves: 4

500 gms mutton, with bone
4 tbsp ghee or oil
2 tbsp powdered green cardamom
3 medium tomatoes, chopped
1 tsp grated ginger
4 green chillies, minced
4 tbsp chopped coriander leaves
1 tsp black pepper powder
½ tsp salt

- Wash meat, pat dry and cut into serving portions.
- Heat ghee or oil in a pan over moderate heat. Add cardamom powder and fry for a moment. Mix in remaining ingredients and cook for about 30 minutes till water from meat has evaporated.
- Add 1½ cups hot water and cover pan. Cook for about 1 hour till meat is tender and gravy thickens.
- Serve with roti.

Note: You can pressure-cook the meat for about 30 minutes. Open cooker and cook uncovered till gravy thickens.

DHAKIYAL CHAPIYOON
Hidden Chops
Serves: 5

10 mutton chops with long projecting bones
250 gms minced mutton
½ tsp salt
1 large potato, boiled, peeled and roughly chopped
1 small onion, roughly chopped
4 green chillies, roughly chopped
4 tbsp chopped coriander leaves
8 mint leaves, chopped
3 bread slices, soaked in water and squeezed dry
½ tsp red chilli powder
1 tbsp coriander-cumin powder
1 tbsp garam masala powder
2 eggs, whisked
2 cups fine breadcrumbs or powdered cornflakes
Oil for shallow frying

Marinade:

1 tsp ginger paste
1 tsp garlic paste
1 tsp salt

- Wash chops and pat dry. Trim and beat with a wooden mallet to break fibres.

- Combine ingredients for marinade, rub into chops and marinate for 30 minutes.

- Steam chops for about 15 minutes till tender and set aside.

- Place mince in a pan with salt and 1½ cups water over high heat. Bring to boil and continue boiling for about

15 minutes till tender and dry. Remove from heat and cool.

- Grind mince with remaining ingredients except chops, eggs, breadcrumbs or cornflakes and oil.

- Coat chops with ground paste, leaving the bone bare. Coat with breadcrumbs or cornflakes, dip in eggs and coat with breadcrumbs or cornflakes again.

- Heat oil in a frying pan and fry chops in batches till golden on both sides. Drain and place on kitchen paper to absorb excess oil.

- Serve hot with a green salad.

Note: Traditionally the chops are held by the bone and eaten with the hands. You may wrap chop bones in foil for easier handling.

TEEVAN JA KABAB
Mutton Kabab
Serves: 4

250 gms minced mutton
2 medium potatoes, peeled and diced
1 small onion, roughly chopped
1 tsp ginger paste
1 tsp garlic paste
4 green chillies, roughly chopped
8 mint leaves, chopped
4 tbsp chopped coriander leaves
2 green cardamoms
2 cloves
½ tsp black cumin seeds (kala jeera)
½ tsp red chilli powder
½ tsp salt
1 egg, whisked
Oil for shallow frying
1 cup fine breadcrumbs or powdered cornflakes

- Place mince and potatoes in a pan with 2 cups water and boil till tender and dry.

- Cool and grind to a paste with remaining ingredients except egg, oil and breadcrumbs or cornflakes.

- Mix in egg and divide into 10 portions. Shape into heart-shaped cutlets.

- Heat oil in a frying pan over moderate heat. Coat cutlets with breadcrumbs or cornflakes and fry in batches till golden on both sides. Drain and place on kitchen paper to absorb excess oil.

- Serve with any chutney of your choice.

The Essential Sindhi Cookbook

ADRUK JOON TIKIYOON
Ginger-flavoured Mutton Cutlets
Serves: 4

These cutlets are supposed to be very good for countering a common cold.

500 gms minced mutton
1 medium onion, minced
4 green chillies, minced
4 tbsp finely chopped coriander leaves
1 tsp black pepper powder
1 tbsp black cumin seeds (kala jeera)
1 tbsp coriander-cumin powder
1 tbsp garam masala powder
1 tsp salt
2 eggs, whisked
4 tbsp oil
3 tbsp ginger paste

- Grind together all ingredients except eggs, oil and ginger. Mix in eggs. Divide into 8-10 portions and form into 2" round cutlets.

- Heat oil in a frying pan over moderate heat. Place cutlets carefully in a layer in pan and fry till base is golden. Turn over carefully and fry the other side till golden. Drain and place on kitchen paper to absorb excess oil.

- Add ginger and ½ cup water to pan, bring to boil and lower heat. Cook till gravy thickens slightly.

- Gently put in cutlets and cook over low heat till all moisture is absorbed.

KHEEMÉ JA KOFTA
Minced Mutton Kofta
Serves: 8

500 gms minced mutton
¾ tsp salt
1 medium onion, roughly chopped
1 tbsp grated ginger
2 green chillies, chopped
2 tbsp chopped coriander leaves
8 mint leaves, chopped
1 tbsp coriander-cumin powder
1 tbsp garam masala powder
2 eggs, whisked
2 cups fine breadcrumbs or powdered cornflakes
Oil for deep frying

Filling:

100 gms grated cottage cheese (paneer)
2 tbsp blanched, peeled and sliced almonds
2 tbsp blanched, peeled and sliced pistachio nuts
¼ tsp saffron strands soaked in ½ tsp hot milk
2 green chillies, minced
2 tbsp chopped coriander leaves
¼ tsp salt

- Place mince in a pan with salt and 1 cup water over high heat. Bring to boil, reduce heat to low and cook for 25 minutes till tender and dry. Remove from heat and cool.

- Grind mince with onion, ginger, green chillies, coriander leaves, mint leaves and spice powders.

- Mix together all ingredients for filling.

- Pinch off lemon-sized balls of mince. Flatten a portion of mince and place 1 tbsp filling in the centre. Work mince around to cover filling completely and shape into an oval kofta. Make remaining kofté in the same way.

- Coat kofté with breadcrumbs or cornflakes, dip in eggs and coat with breadcrumbs or cornflakes again.

- Heat oil in a kadhai or deep frying pan over moderate heat and fry kofté in batches till golden brown. Drain and place on kitchen paper to absorb excess oil.

- Serve hot with any chutney of your choice.

SEYAL TEEVAN
Onion-flavoured Mutton Curry
Serves: 8

500 gms mutton, with bone
6 tbsp ghee or oil
4 large onions, minced
3 medium tomatoes, chopped
1 tbsp ginger paste
1 tbsp garlic paste
4 green chillies, minced
4 tbsp chopped coriander leaves
6 mint leaves, chopped
6 curry leaves
½ tsp turmeric powder
1 tsp red chilli powder
1 tbsp coriander-cumin powder
1 tsp garam masala powder
½ tsp salt
½ cup curd, whisked
¼ cup brandy (optional)

- Wash meat, pat dry and cut into serving portions.

- Heat ghee or oil in a pan over low heat. Add remaining ingredients and cover pan. Cook without adding any water for 45 minutes till meat is tender and gravy thickens.

- Serve with jowar jo dhodho (p. 182).

Note: You can pressure-cook the meat for 30 minutes. Open cooker and cook uncovered till gravy thickens.

BHUGAL TEEVAN
Mutton-fry
Serves: 4

500 gms boneless mutton
4 tbsp ghee or oil

Ground to a smooth paste:
½ cup sour curd, whisked
1 medium onion, roughly chopped
1 tsp grated ginger
1 tsp minced garlic
4 green chillies, roughly chopped
3 tbsp chopped coriander leaves
8 mint leaves, chopped
½ tsp red chilli powder
1 tsp coriander-cumin powder
1 tsp garam masala powder
½ tsp salt

- Wash meat, pat dry and cut into serving portions.

- Mix spice paste into meat and set aside to marinate for about 30 minutes.

- Heat ghee or oil in a pan over low heat. Stir in meat with its marinade and cover pan. Cook without adding any water for about 45 minutes till tender and dry.

- Serve with roti.

RAAN
Roast Leg of Mutton
Serves: 12

This is a very famous dish from Sindh and was served by the zamindars. No special occasion was complete without raan and mutton biryani.

1½ kg leg of mutton, kept whole
2 tsp red chilli powder
2 tsp ginger powder (saunth)
1 tsp turmeric powder
1 tbsp coriander-cumin powder
¼ tsp grated nutmeg
¼ tsp powdered mace
1½ tsp salt
½ tsp saffron strands soaked in 3 tbsp hot milk
1¼ cups ghee
½ tsp asafoetida powder (hing)
4 cups curd, whisked

Spice paste:

1" stick cinnamon
4 cloves
10 black peppercorns
4 black cardamoms
4 green cardamoms
2 tsp aniseed (saunf)
2 tbsp poppy seeds (khus-khus)
2 bay leaves (tej patta)
2 tbsp cashewnuts
2 tbsp almonds, blanched and peeled
¼ copra, grated
2 tbsp sultanas (kishmish)

Ground to a smooth paste:

> 2 medium onions, roughly chopped
> 1 tbsp ginger paste
> 1 tbsp garlic paste

Garnish:

> 6 sheets silver leaf (chandi ka varq)

- Heat a tava or griddle over moderate heat and roast whole spices, bay leaves, nuts and copra for spice paste individually for a few moments till fragrant. Add sultanas and grind to a smooth paste without water.

- Wash leg and pat dry. Make deep gashes in the flesh all over the leg with a sharp knife and set aside.

- Mix spice paste with spice powders, salt, saffron with its soaking liquid and onion paste. Rub paste all over leg and set aside to marinate for about 1 hour.

- Heat ghee in a pan without handles and large enough to hold the leg. Remove from heat and place leg in pan. Dissolve asafoetida in ¼ cup hot water, mix with curd and pour over leg.

- Cover pan tightly and roast in an oven preheated to 200°C (400°F) for 1½ hours. (Cover pan with aluminium foil if the lid does not fit tightly enough.)

- Remove cover and roast uncovered for 35 minutes longer, basting every 5-7 minutes with gravy from pan.

- Garnish with silver leaf and serve with teevan ji biryani (p. 150).

Note: You can garnish the leg with sultanas and shredded almonds along with the silver leaf.

MAGAZ JI CURRY
Brain Curry
Serves: 4

2 goat's brains
4 tbsp ghee
1 tomato, puréed
½ tsp red chilli powder
½ tsp black pepper powder
1 tbsp coriander-cumin powder
1 tsp garam masala powder
¾ tsp salt
2 medium potatoes, peeled and cubed
1 cup shelled green peas

Ground to a paste:
1 large onion, roughly chopped
1 tsp grated ginger

Garnish:
2 tbsp chopped coriander leaves

- Prepare brains and boil as given on p. 29. Cut into 2" cubes.

- Heat ghee in a frying pan over low heat. Add brains and fry for about 5 minutes on each side till golden. Drain and set aside.

- Add onion paste to pan and fry till golden. Mix in tomato, spice powders and salt. Cook for about 5 minutes till well blended. Add potatoes, green peas and 1 cup water. Simmer till vegetables are tender.

- Gently stir in brains and simmer for 5 minutes longer.

- Garnish with coriander leaves and serve hot with roti.

PHOTAN MEIN MAGAZ
Cardamom-flavoured Brain Curry
Serves: 4

2 goat's brains
4 tbsp ghee or oil
1 medium tomato, puréed
1 tsp black pepper powder
1 tbsp powdered green cardamom
1 tbsp coriander-cumin powder
¾ tsp salt

Garnish:

2 tbsp chopped coriander leaves
2 green chillies, minced

- Prepare brains and boil as given on p. 29. Cut into 2" cubes.

- Heat ghee or oil in a frying pan over moderate heat. Add brains and fry for about 5 minutes on each side till golden. Drain and set aside.

- Add tomato, spice powders and salt to pan. Cook for about 5 minutes till well blended. Gently mix in brains and simmer for a few minutes longer.

- Garnish with coriander leaves and green chillies and serve hot with roti.

MAGAZ JO KHEEMO
Minced Brains
Serves: 4

2 goat's brains
4 tbsp ghee or oil
1 large tomato, chopped
2 green chillies, minced
½ tsp red chilli powder
½ tsp black pepper powder
1 tsp coriander-cumin powder
1 tsp garam masala powder
¾ tsp salt

Ground to a paste:

1 medium onion, roughly chopped
1 tsp grated ginger

Garnish:

2 tbsp chopped coriander leaves
2 green chillies, chopped

- Prepare brains and boil as given on p. 29. Cut into 2" cubes.

- Heat ghee or oil in a frying pan over moderate heat. Add brains and fry for about 5 minutes on each side, till golden. Drain and set aside.

- Add onion paste to pan and fry till golden. Blend in tomato, green chillies, spice powders and salt. Cook for about 5 minutes till well blended and thick.

- Add brains and mix well. Cut brains in the pan with a knife till they resemble mince.

- Garnish with coriander leaves and green chillies and serve hot with roti.

DAG MEIN MAGAZ
Onion-flavoured Brains
Serves: 4

2 goat's brains
3 tbsp ghee or oil
1 medium onion, minced
½ tsp grated ginger
1 medium tomato, diced
4 tbsp curd, whisked
¼ tsp turmeric powder
½ tsp red chilli powder
1 tsp coriander-cumin powder
½ tsp garam masala powder
¾ tsp salt

Ground to a paste:
2 tbsp chopped coriander leaves
5 mint leaves, chopped
2 green chillies, roughly chopped

- Prepare brains and boil as given on p. 29. Cut into 2" cubes.

- Heat ghee in a frying pan over moderate heat. Add onion and ginger and fry till onion turns translucent. Mix in remaining ingredients except brains. Cook for about 5 minutes, till well blended.

- Gently mix in brains and simmer for 5 minutes longer till gravy thickens.

- Serve hot with roti.

BHUGAL JERANDI
Curried Kidneys and Liver
Serves: 4

500 gms mixed kidneys and liver
1 tsp salt
4 tbsp ghee or oil
2 medium onions, finely sliced
2 medium tomatoes, blanched, peeled and diced
½ tsp red chilli powder
1 tbsp coriander-cumin powder
½ tsp garam masala powder
4 green chillies, minced

Marinade:

1 tbsp grated ginger
1 tbsp minced garlic
½ tsp turmeric powder
¾ tsp salt

Garnish:

2 tbsp chopped coriander leaves

- Wash kidneys and liver thoroughly under running water.

- Place in a pan with salt and water to cover and soak for about 15 minutes. Drain and remove membranes, threads and fat. Rinse well and drain. Cut into 2" cubes.

- Combine ingredients for marinade, rub into kidneys and liver and marinate for 30 minutes.

- Place kidneys and liver in a pan with 2 cups water over high heat and boil for about 10 minutes till tender and dry.

- Heat ghee or oil in a pan over moderate heat. Add onions and fry till translucent.

- Mix in tomatoes and spice powders and cook till well blended. Add green chillies, kidneys and liver with 4 tbsp water and simmer for 5-7 minutes till gravy thickens.

- Garnish with coriander leaves and serve hot with roti.

Note: Do not overcook the kidneys and liver, otherwise they will turn hard.

Variation: You can prepare fish roe (a great delicacy in Sindh) in the same way. Do not boil the roe, but fry it in 2 tbsp ghee or oil.

JERANDI DAHI MEIN
Kidneys and Liver in a Curd-based Curry
Serves: 4

500 gms mixed kidneys and liver
1 tsp + 1 tsp salt
4 tbsp ghee or oil
2 large onions, finely chopped
1 tbsp ginger paste
1 tbsp garlic paste
½ tsp red chilli powder
1 tbsp coriander-cumin powder
1 tsp garam masala powder
2 medium tomatoes, chopped
2 tbsp chopped coriander leaves
½ cup curd, whisked

- Wash kidneys and liver thoroughly under running water.

- Place in a pan with 1 tsp salt and water to cover and soak for about 15 minutes. Drain and remove membranes, threads and fat. Rinse well and drain. Cut into 2" cubes.

- Heat ghee or oil in a pan over moderate heat. Add onions, ginger and garlic and fry till onions turn translucent.

- Mix in kidneys, liver, spice powders and 1 tsp salt and simmer for about 15 minutes till dry.

- Blend in remaining ingredients and cook for about 10 minutes, till kidneys and liver are tender and ghee or oil rises to the surface.

- Serve hot with roti.

Chicken

SEYAL MURGI
Chicken in an Onion Gravy
Serves: 6

1 chicken (about 1 kg)
5 tbsp ghee
1" stick cinnamon, broken
6 cloves
4 black cardamoms
1½ cups curd, whisked
4 green chillies, minced
½ tsp red chilli powder
1 tbsp coriander-cumin powder
1 tsp garam masala powder
1½ tsp salt

Ground to a paste:
4 large onions, roughly chopped
1 tbsp ginger paste
1 tbsp garlic paste

Garnish:
4 tbsp chopped coriander leaves

- Joint chicken, wash and drain.
- Heat ghee in a large pan over moderate heat. Add whole spices and fry for a few moments till fragrant.
- Stir in onion paste and fry till golden. Add chicken and fry stirring occasionally till brown.
- Mix in curd, green chillies, spice powders and salt and cover pan with a tight-fitting lid. Cook over low heat for about 30 minutes till chicken is tender and gravy thickens.
- Garnish with coriander leaves and serve hot with roti.

SAI BHAAJI MEIN MURGI
Chicken with Spinach
Serves: 5

1 chicken (about 1 kg)
500 gms spinach
5 tbsp ghee or oil
2 large tomatoes, puréed
4 green chillies, minced
1 tsp turmeric powder
1½ tsp red chilli powder
1 tbsp coriander-cumin powder
1 tbsp garam masala powder
1½ tsp salt

Ground to a paste:
2 medium onions, roughly chopped
1 tbsp ginger paste
1 tbsp garlic paste

Garnish:
½ cup cream (optional)
4 tbsp chopped coriander leaves

- Joint chicken, wash and drain.

- Pluck spinach leaves, wash thoroughly, drain well and chop finely.

- Heat ghee or oil in a large pan over moderate heat. Add onion paste and fry till golden. Mix in spinach and cook over low heat for about 10 minutes till dry.

- Add remaining ingredients except garnish and mix well.

- Cover pan with a tight-fitting lid and cook over low heat for about 30 minutes till chicken is tender. Stir occasionally and add a little water if necessary.

- Garnish with cream (if used) and coriander leaves and serve hot with rice.

KARÉ MIRCH JI MURGI
Pepper Chicken
Serves: 5

1 chicken (about 1 kg)
5 tbsp ghee
3 tbsp black pepper powder
2 tbsp powdered green cardamoms
1½ tsp salt
3 medium tomatoes, blanched, peeled and puréed
4 tbsp chopped coriander leaves

- Joint chicken, wash and drain.

- Heat ghee in a large pan over moderate heat. Add chicken, spice powders and salt and fry stirring frequently till brown.

- Stir in remaining ingredients and cover pan with a tight-fitting lid. Cook over low heat for about 30 minutes till chicken is tender and dry.

- Serve hot with roti.

TAMATAN MEIN MURGI
Tomato Chicken
Serves: 5

1 chicken (about 1 kg)
6 tbsp butter
4 large tomatoes, puréed
4 green chillies, minced
4 tbsp chopped coriander leaves
1½ tsp red chilli powder
1 tsp coriander-cumin powder
1 tsp garam masala powder

Marinade:

1 tsp ginger paste
1 tsp garlic paste
½ tsp turmeric powder
1½ tsp salt

- Joint chicken, wash and pat dry. Make fine gashes in the flesh with a knife.

- Combine ingredients for marinade, rub into chicken and marinate for 30 minutes.

- Heat butter in a large pan over moderate heat. Add chicken and fry stirring frequently till brown.

- Mix in remaining ingredients and cover pan. Cook over low heat for about 30 minutes till chicken is tender and gravy thickens.

- Serve hot with any pulao of your choice.

TARIYAL MURGI
Fried Chicken
Serves: 4

1 chicken (about 1 kg)
6 tbsp ghee or oil
2 medium onions, minced
1 tsp ginger paste
1 tsp garlic paste
4 green chillies, finely chopped
2 fresh red chillies, finely chopped
1 cup curd, whisked
2 medium tomatoes, puréed
4 tbsp chopped coriander leaves
1 tbsp coriander-cumin powder
1 tbsp garam masala powder
1½ tsp salt

- Joint chicken, wash and pat dry.

- Heat ghee or oil in a large pan over moderate heat. Add onions, ginger, garlic and chillies and fry till onions turn golden.

- Add chicken and fry turning frequently till brown.

- Stir in remaining ingredients and cover pan. Cook over low heat for about 30 minutes till chicken is tender and ghee or oil rises to the surface.

- Serve hot with any pulao of your choice.

DAHI MEIN MURGI
Chicken in a Curd-based Curry
Serves: 6

1 chicken (about 1 kg)
5 tbsp ghee or oil
4 large onions, finely sliced
1 tbsp minced ginger
1 tbsp minced garlic
½ tsp turmeric powder
1½ tsp red chilli powder
1½ tsp salt
1 cup curd, whisked
4 green chillies, minced
4 medium tomatoes, chopped
1 small unripe mango, peeled and sliced (optional)
4 tbsp chopped coriander leaves
8 curry leaves, chopped
8 mint leaves, chopped
250 gms baby potatoes, peeled
4 tbsp brandy (optional)

Ground to a fine powder:
½" stick cinnamon
3 cloves
3 green cardamoms
½ tsp black peppercorns
1 tbsp coriander seeds
½ tsp cumin seeds
½ tsp black cumin seeds (kala jeera)
4 bay leaves (tej patta)

- Joint chicken, wash and drain.

- Heat ghee or oil in a large pan over moderate heat. Add onions, ginger and garlic and fry till onions turn golden.

- Add chicken and fry stirring occasionally till brown.

- Stir in remaining ingredients except potatoes and brandy. Cook for about 5 minutes till well blended.

- Mix in potatoes, brandy (if used) and 2 cups hot water. Cook for 15-20 minutes till chicken is tender and dry.

- Serve hot with roti.

BHARIYAL MURGI
Stuffed Chicken
Serves: 6

1 chicken (about 1 kg), kept whole
2" piece ginger, crushed
1½ tsp salt
6 tbsp butter
500 gms baby potatoes, boiled and peeled
5 tbsp ghee
1 cup thick tamarind juice

Ground to a paste:
5 green cardamoms
4 cloves
1 tsp black peppercorns
1 tbsp coriander seeds
2 bay leaves (tej patta)
4 dry red Kashmir chillies
4 green chillies
4 tbsp chopped coriander leaves

- Wash chicken thoroughly and pat dry. Prick chicken all over with a fork.

- Mix ginger with salt and rub into chicken. Set aside to marinate for 4-5 hours in the refrigerator.

- Mix ground spices with butter and rub a portion of it into chicken.

- Mix potatoes with remaining spice paste and butter and fill into chicken cavity. Sew the opening with cotton thread.

- Heat ghee in a large pan over moderate heat. Add

chicken and fry turning frequently till well browned.

- Pour in tamarind juice and 1 cup hot water and cover pan with a tight-fitting lid. Cook over low heat for about 30 minutes till chicken is tender and gravy thickens.

- Serve hot with bhaajiyoon jo pulao (p. 146).

BADAMIYOON MEIN MURGI
Almond Chicken
Serves: 4

1 chicken (about 1 kg), kept whole
6 tbsp melted butter
½ tsp saffron strands soaked in 1 tbsp hot milk
1½ tsp salt

Ground to a paste:
½" stick cinnamon
4 cloves
2 bay leaves (tej patta)
4 green cardamoms
1 tsp cumin seeds
1 tsp black cumin seeds (kala jeera)
4 dry red Kashmir chillies
1 cup ground almonds
1 tbsp grated ginger
1 tbsp minced garlic

Garnish:
2 tbsp chopped coriander leaves

- Wash chicken thoroughly and pat dry. Prick chicken all over with a fork. Mix butter, saffron, salt and ground paste with 6 tbsp water. Rub into chicken and marinate for 30 minutes.

- Place chicken in a roasting pan and pour marinade over it. Roast in an oven preheated to 180°C (350°F) for 1 hour till tender.

- Garnish with coriander leaves and serve with teevan ji biryani (p. 150).

Dal

THOOMAWARI DAL
Garlic Dal
Serves: 4

1 heaped cup husked Egyptian lentils (masoor dal)
½ tsp turmeric powder
½ tsp salt
2 tbsp ghee
½ tsp cumin seeds
¼ tsp asafoetida powder (hing)
1 tsp ginger paste
1 tsp garlic paste
8 curry leaves
2 tbsp chopped coriander leaves
4 green chillies, slit
2 medium tomatoes, puréed

- Wash dal, soak in water for 1 hour and drain.

- Place dal in a pan with turmeric, salt and 2½ cups water over high heat. Bring to boil, lower heat and cook for about 15-20 minutes till soft. Remove from heat, mash and set aside.

- Heat ghee in a large pan over moderate heat and add cumin seeds and asafoetida. When cumin seeds stop spluttering, add ginger and garlic and stir-fry for a few moments.

- Add remaining ingredients except dal and mix well. Cook for about 5 minutes till well blended.

- Stir in dal and heat through.

- Serve with rice.

ANIYOON JI CURRY
Bengal Gram Fritters in a Spicy Curry
Serves: 4

Fritters:

1 cup gram flour (besan)
2 green chillies, minced
1 tsp minced ginger
1 tsp cumin seeds
1 tsp crushed pomegranate seeds (anardana)
¼ tsp salt

Curry:

2 tbsp oil
1 large onion, minced
1 tsp minced ginger
1 tsp minced garlic
4 green chillies, slit
½ tsp red chilli powder
1 tbsp mango powder (amchur)
1 tbsp coriander-cumin powder
½ tsp garam masala powder
¼ tsp salt

Tempering:

1 tbsp oil
¼ tsp mustard seeds
¼ tsp cumin seeds
A pinch asafoetida powder (hing)

Garnish:

2 tbsp chopped coriander leaves

• Combine all ingredients for fritters in a bowl and mix well. Add ¼ cup water, a little at a time, and knead to make a stiff dough.

- Roll out on a floured surface into a ¼" thin sheet. Cut into 1" square pieces.

- Heat 2½ cups water in a large pan and bring to boil. Add gram flour squares and boil for 20 minutes. Drain and set aside. Reserve water.

- Heat oil for curry in a large pan over moderate heat. Add onion, ginger and garlic and fry till onion turns translucent.

- Stir in green chillies, spice powders, salt, fritters and reserved water. Cover pan and cook over low heat for 5-7 minutes till gravy thickens.

- Heat oil for tempering in a small pan over moderate heat and add remaining ingredients for tempering. When mustard seeds stop spluttering, pour contents of pan over curry.

- Garnish with coriander leaves and serve hot with roti or rice.

KHATTI DAL
Tangy Dal
Serves: 4

1 heaped cup husked Bengal gram (chana dal)
2 tbsp ghee
2 medium onions, minced
1 tsp ginger paste
1 tsp garlic paste
4 + 4 green chillies, minced
½ tsp turmeric powder
1 tbsp coriander-cumin powder
½ tsp salt
1 large tomato, blanched, peeled and sliced
4 tbsp thick tamarind juice

Tempering:

1 tbsp ghee or oil
1 tsp cumin seeds

Garnish:

2 tbsp chopped coriander leaves

- Wash dal, soak in water for 1 hour and drain.

- Heat ghee in a large pan over moderate heat. Add onions, ginger, garlic and 4 green chillies and fry till onions turn translucent.

- Add dal with spice powders, salt and 2½ cups water. Raise heat and bring to boil. Lower heat, cover pan and cook over low heat for 30 minutes till dal is soft. Remove from heat.

- Mash dal lightly and return to heat. Add 4 green chillies, tomato and tamarind and cook for about 5 minutes.

- Heat ghee or oil for tempering in a small pan over moderate heat and add cumin seeds. When they stop spluttering, pour contents of pan over dal.

- Garnish with coriander leaves and serve with pakwan (p. 178).

KOKUMWARI DAL
Dal with Kokum
Serves: 4

1 cup pigeon peas (arhar/toover)
1 tsp turmeric powder
½ tsp salt
12-15 kokum (p. 233)
1 tsp minced ginger
4 green chillies, slit
2 tbsp chopped coriander leaves
8 curry leaves

Tempering:

3 tbsp ghee
½ tsp mustard seeds
½ tsp fenugreek seeds (methi)
½ tsp cumin seeds
¼ tsp asafoetida powder (hing)

- Wash dal, soak in water for 1 hour and drain.

- Place dal in a pan with turmeric, salt and 2½ cups water over high heat. Bring to boil, lower heat and cook for about 30 minutes till soft. Remove from heat.

- Mash dal and return to heat. Stir in remaining ingredients except tempering. Pour in 1 cup water and cook over low heat for about 10 minutes.

- Heat ghee for tempering in a small pan over moderate heat and add remaining ingredients for tempering. When mustard seeds stop spluttering, pour contents of pan over dal.

- Serve with rice.

MAKHANI DAL
Butter Dal
Serves: 5

1 heaped cup husked green beans (moong dal)
½ tsp turmeric powder
½ tsp salt
¼ tsp red chilli powder
¼ tsp black pepper powder
½ tsp mango powder (amchur)
5 tbsp butter
½ tsp cumin seeds
1 medium onion, minced
1 medium tomato, finely chopped
4 green chillies, minced
2 tbsp chopped coriander leaves
1 tsp minced ginger

- Wash dal, soak in water for 1 hour and drain.

- Place dal in a pressure cooker with turmeric, salt and 1½ cups water. Cook under pressure for 5 minutes. Remove from heat and place cooker under running water to reduce pressure immediately. The grains should be tender but separate.

- Transfer dal to a serving dish. Mix together remaining spice powders and sprinkle over dal.

- Melt butter in a pan over low heat and add cumin seeds. When they stop spluttering, add remaining ingredients except dal. Fry for 1 minute and pour contents of pan over dal.

- Serve with plain poori (p. 179).

PANCHRATNI DAL
Five-jewel Dal
Serves: 5

2½ tbsp husked Bengal gram (chana dal)
2½ tbsp green beans (moong dal)
2½ tbsp Egyptian lentils (masoor dal)
2½ tbsp black beans (urad dal)
2½ tbsp pigeon peas (arhar/toover)
½ tsp turmeric powder
½ tsp salt
2 tbsp ghee
4 green chillies, slit
2 large tomatoes, blanched, peeled and puréed
1 large tomato, finely sliced
1 small onion, minced
½ tsp grated ginger
3 tbsp chopped coriander leaves

Tempering:

2 tbsp ghee
1 tsp cumin seeds
¼ tsp asafoetida powder (hing)

- Wash dals, soak in water for 1 hour and drain.

- Place dals in a large pan with turmeric, salt and 2½ cups water over high heat. Bring to boil, lower heat and cover pan. Simmer for about 30 minutes till soft.

- Heat ghee in a large pan over low heat. Add green chillies and puréed tomatoes. Cook for about 5 minutes till well blended and slightly thick.

- Mix in dals, cook for a few minutes longer and remove from heat.

- Heat ghee for tempering in a pan over moderate heat and add cumin seeds and asafoetida. When cumin seeds stop spluttering, add sliced tomato, onion, ginger and coriander leaves. Fry for 3-4 minutes and pour contents of pan over dal.

- Serve with roti or jowar jo dhodho (p. 182).

TRIDALI
Three-jewel Dal
Serves: 5

4 tbsp red kidney beans (rajma)
4 tbsp husked black beans (urad dal)
4 tbsp husked Bengal gram (chana dal)
¼ tsp turmeric powder
¾ tsp salt
4 tbsp butter
1 tsp cumin seeds
1 small onion, minced
½ tsp ginger paste
½ tsp garlic paste
2 green chillies, minced
2 medium tomatoes, puréed
½ tsp coriander-cumin powder
½ tsp garam masala powder

Garnish:

4 tbsp cream
2 tbsp chopped coriander leaves

- Wash kidney beans and dals and soak in water for 4-5 hours.

- Drain kidney beans and dals, rinse and place in a pan with turmeric, salt and 3 cups water over high heat. Bring to boil, lower heat and cook for 30 minutes till tender.

- Melt butter in a large pan over low heat and add cumin seeds. When they stop spluttering, add onion, ginger, garlic and green chillies. Fry till onion turns translucent.

- Stir in tomatoes and cook stirring occasionally for about 5 minutes.

- Mix in dal with remaining spice powders. Cook over low heat for about 5 minutes till thick.

- Transfer dal to a serving dish and pour cream over it. Garnish with coriander leaves and serve with roti or jowar jo dhodho (p. 182).

Rice

METHI JO PULAO
Fenugreek Leaf Pulao
Serves: 5

2 cups long-grained rice
4 tbsp ghee or oil
10 cloves garlic, kept whole
4 green chillies, minced
2 cups (100 gms) chopped fenugreek leaves (methi)
¼ cup chopped coriander leaves
8 mint leaves, chopped
2 large tomatoes, puréed
1 tsp cumin seeds
½ tsp turmeric powder
½ tsp red chilli powder
1 tbsp coriander-cumin powder
1 tsp salt

- Wash rice and soak in water for 30 minutes.

- Heat ghee or oil in a large pan over low heat. Add garlic and fry stirring continuously for a few moments.

- Mix in green chillies, fenugreek, coriander and mint leaves. Cook over low heat stirring occasionally for about 5 minutes till moisture has evaporated.

- Stir in tomatoes, cumin seeds, spice powders and salt. Cook for about 5 minutes longer till gravy thickens.

- Drain rice and stir into pan with 4 cups water. Bring to boil, lower heat and cover pan. Simmer till rice is cooked and grains remain separate.

- Serve with seasoned curd and fried papad or kheecha (p. 208).

141

BHUGAL CHAWAR
Brown Rice
Serves: 4

2 cups long-grained rice
3 tbsp oil
1" stick cinnamon
4 cloves
2 green cardamoms
4 bay leaves (tej patta)
3 dry red chillies
2 large onions, minced
1 tsp minced ginger
3 green chillies, minced
2 tbsp chopped coriander leaves
½ tsp red chilli powder
1 tsp garam masala powder
1 tsp coriander-cumin powder
1 tsp salt

Garnish:

1 tbsp ghee
1 tsp black cumin seeds (kala jeera)

- Wash rice and soak in water for 30 minutes.

- Heat oil in a large pan over moderate heat. Add whole spices, bay leaves and red chillies and fry for a few moments till fragrant.

- Add onions, ginger and green chillies and fry stirring frequently till onions turn golden brown.

- Drain rice and stir into pan with coriander leaves, spice powders, salt and 4 cups water. Bring to boil, lower heat and cover pan. Simmer till rice is cooked and grains remain separate. Transfer to a serving dish.

- Heat ghee for garnish in a small pan and sprinkle over rice with black cumin.

- Serve hot with sai bhaaji (p. 58) and patatan joon chapiyoon (p. 160).

KHICHDI
Rice with Green Beans
Serves: 6

Sindhi khichdi is a little watery in texture and the grains should not be too dry after cooking.

2 cups long-grained rice
1 cup husked green beans (moong dal)
½ tsp turmeric powder
1 tsp salt
4 tbsp hot ghee

- Wash rice and dal, soak in water for 30 minutes and drain.

- Place all ingredients except ghee in a large pan with 5½ cups water. Place pan over high heat and bring to boil. Lower heat and cover pan. Simmer till rice and dal are cooked, but the dish is still a little watery.

- Pour hot ghee over khichdi and serve with curd, roasted papad and sai chutney (p. 226).

VADIYOON JO PULAO
Pulao with Lentil Cakes
Serves: 5

2 cups long-grained rice
5 tbsp oil
8 lentil cakes (moong dal vadi, commercially available)
1" stick cinnamon, broken
4 cloves
3 green cardamoms
2 bay leaves (tej patta)
1 medium onion, minced
1 tsp minced ginger
½ tsp turmeric powder
1 tsp red chilli powder
1½ tsp salt
2 large tomatoes, puréed
1 cup shelled green peas
3 tbsp chopped coriander leaves

Garnish:
2 medium potatoes, peeled and cut into finger chips
1 tbsp ghee
1 tsp black cumin seeds (kala jeera)
10 cashewnuts, lightly fried
10 sultanas (kishmish), lightly fried

- Wash rice and soak in water for 30 minutes.

- Heat oil in a large pan over moderate heat. Add potatoes for garnish and fry till tender and golden. Drain and place on kitchen paper to absorb excess oil.

- Add vadi to pan and fry till golden. Drain and place on kitchen paper to absorb excess oil.

- Add whole spices and bay leaves to pan and fry for a

few moments till fragrant.

- Add onion and ginger and fry till onion turns golden.

- Mix in vadi, spice powders, salt, tomatoes and green peas. Cook over low heat for about 5 minutes till gravy thickens.

- Drain rice and stir into pan with coriander leaves and 4 cups water. Bring to boil, lower heat and cover pan. Simmer over low heat for about 10 minutes till rice is cooked and grains remain separate.

- Transfer rice to a serving dish. Heat ghee in a small pan and sprinkle over rice with black cumin.

- Garnish with potatoes, cashewnuts and sultanas and serve.

BHAAJIYOON JO PULAO
Vegetable Pulao
Serves: 5

2 cups long-grained rice
500 gms mixed vegetables—potatoes, carrots, capsicums and
cauliflower
4 tbsp + 2 tbsp ghee
1 cup shelled green peas
½ tsp turmeric powder
1 tsp coriander-cumin powder
1 tsp garam masala powder
2 large tomatoes, blanched, peeled and puréed
1 tsp julienned ginger
1" stick cinnamon, broken
2 cloves
3 green cardamoms
3 bay leaves (tej patta)
1½ tsp salt
1 cup curd, whisked

Garnish:

4 thick green chillies, slit and lightly fried
3 tbsp chopped coriander leaves

- Wash rice and soak in water for 30 minutes.

- Peel and cut potatoes into cubes.

- Scrape carrots. Remove pith and seeds of capsicums.
  Cut carrots and capsicums into strips.

- Cut cauliflower into florets and wash.

- Heat 4 tbsp ghee in a large pan over moderate heat.
  Add all vegetables and stir-fry for about 5 minutes.

- Blend in spice powders, tomatoes and ginger. Cook

for about 5 minutes till vegetables are tender. Remove from heat and keep warm.

- Heat 2 tbsp ghee in another large pan over moderate heat. Add whole spices and bay leaves and fry for a few moments till fragrant.

- Drain rice and stir into pan with salt and 4 cups water. Bring to boil, lower heat and cover pan. Simmer till rice is cooked and grains remain separate.

- Spread half the rice on a serving platter. Spoon curd over it. Arrange vegetables over curd and spread remaining rice on top.

- Garnish with green chillies and coriander leaves and serve with fried papad.

MACHHI JO PULAO
Fish Pulao
Serves: 4

2 cups long-grained rice
1 medium pomfret (500 gms), sliced through the bone
4 tbsp oil
3 medium onions, minced
1 tsp ginger paste
1 tsp garlic paste
2 large tomatoes, puréed
1 tsp cumin seeds
1 tsp red chilli powder
1 tsp coriander-cumin powder
3 tbsp chopped coriander leaves
1 tsp salt

Marinade:

½ tsp turmeric powder
½ tsp salt
2 tbsp lime juice

Garnish:

1 tsp garam masala powder

- Wash rice and soak in water for 30 minutes.

- Wash fish well and pat dry. Combine ingredients for marinade, rub into fish and marinate for 30 minutes.

- Heat oil in a large pan over moderate heat. Add onions, ginger and garlic and fry till onions turn golden.

- Blend in tomatoes, cumin seeds and spice powders and lower heat. Cook for about 5 minutes stirring occasionally till well blended.

- Add fish and 1½ cups hot water. Mix gently and simmer for about 5 minutes till fish is tender and gravy thickens.

- Stir in coriander leaves. Carefully remove fish slices and half the gravy from pan and set aside.

- Drain rice and stir into pan with salt and 4 cups water. Bring to boil, lower heat and cover pan. Simmer till rice is almost cooked and dry.

- Arrange fish slices over rice and spread reserved gravy over them. Cover pan with a tight-fitting lid. Simmer over very low heat till rice is cooked and grains remain separate.

- Sprinkle garam masala on top and serve with seasoned curd.

TEEVAN JI BIRYANI
Mutton Biryani
Serves: 6

This biryani is served on every special occasion along with raan.

250 gms mixed kidneys and liver
1 tsp + 1 tsp salt
250 gms mutton with bones
2 cups long-grained rice
1 cup ghee or oil
4 green cardamoms
4 cloves
4 bay leaves (tej patta)
1 tbsp red chilli powder
¼ cup brandy (optional)
1 tbsp coriander-cumin powder
1 tsp garam masala powder
A few drops orange, red and green food colour (optional)
½ tsp saffron strands soaked in 2 tbsp hot milk

Ground to a smooth paste:

2 large onions, minced
1 tbsp ginger paste
1 tbsp garlic paste
4 green chillies, roughly chopped
½ cup chopped coriander leaves
¼ cup chopped mint leaves

Marinade:

1 cup curd, whisked
4 medium tomatoes, chopped
½ tsp salt

4 tbsp blanched, peeled and sliced almonds
4 tbsp blanched, peeled and sliced pistachio nuts
Dry rose petals

- Wash kidneys and liver thoroughly under running water.

- Place in a pan with 1 tsp salt and water to cover and soak for about 15 minutes. Drain and remove membranes, threads and fat. Rinse well, drain and pat dry. Cut into 1" cubes.

- Wash meat, drain, pat dry and cut into serving portions.

- Combine ground paste with marinade in a bowl. Add kidneys, liver and meat and mix well. Set aside to marinate for about 5 hours.

- Wash rice and soak in water for 30 minutes.

- Heat ghee or oil in a large pan over moderate heat. Add whole spices and bay leaves and fry for a few moments till fragrant.

- Mix in kidneys, liver and meat with their marinade, chilli powder and brandy (if used). Cover pan and cook over low heat for 35-40 minutes till meat and offals are tender and gravy thickens.

- Place a pan with 4 cups water and 1 tsp salt over high heat and bring to boil. Drain rice and stir into pan. Bring to boil, lower heat and cover pan. Simmer for about 15 minutes till rice is almost cooked and dry.

- Sprinkle in remaining spice powders and mix gently with a fork.

- Divide rice into 4 portions. If using food colours, mix each colour with about ¼ tsp water. Sprinkle 3 portions of rice with the different food colours and mix gently with a fork.

- Grease a large pan and arrange alternate layers of rice and meat, starting and ending with rice.

- Cover with a tight-fitting lid and cook over very low heat till rice is tender and dry. (Cover pan with aluminium foil if the lid does not fit tightly enough and place pan on a tava over low heat if your stove does not give you very low heat.)

- Spoon biryani into a serving platter, sprinkle saffron with its soaking liquid on top, garnish with nuts and rose petals and serve with raan (p. 104).

Note: Use food colour from a recognized and reputed brand.

Snacks

SANNA PAKODA
Gram Flour Fritters
Serves: 5

Sindhis love to eat these pakodé with one-day-old phulko.

1 cup gram flour (besan)
¼ tsp salt
A large pinch sodium bicarbonate
1 tsp cumin seeds
1 tsp coarsely crushed pomegranate seeds (anardana)
1 large onion, minced
4 green chillies, minced
4 tbsp chopped coriander leaves
Oil for deep frying

- Combine all ingredients except oil in a bowl and mix well. Add about ¼ cup water, a little at a time, and mix to make a thick batter of dropping consistency.

- Heat oil in a kadhai or deep frying pan to smoking point over high heat. Lower heat to moderate and drop teaspoons of batter into oil. Fry pakodé in batches till light gold. Drain and place on kitchen paper to absorb excess oil till cool.

- Break pakodé into pieces.

- Reheat oil and fry pakodé till crisp and golden. Drain and place on kitchen paper to absorb excess oil.

Note: You can fry the pakodé up to the light-gold stage and store in the refrigerator for up to a week. Break and fry again when required.

155

BHAAJIYOON JA PAKODA
Vegetable Fritters
Serves: 5

2 cups gram flour (besan)
A large pinch sodium bicarbonate
¼ cup chopped spinach leaves
1 cup mixed finely chopped vegetables—potatoes, aubergines
(baingan) and cauliflower
4 green chillies, minced
1 tsp grated ginger
1½ tsp salt
2 tbsp chopped coriander leaves
Oil for deep frying

- Combine all ingredients except oil in a bowl and mix well. Add about ½ cup water, a little at a time, and mix to make a thick batter of dropping consistency.

- Heat oil in a kadhai or deep frying pan to smoking point over high heat. Lower heat to moderate and drop teaspoons of batter into oil. Fry pakodé in batches till light gold. Drain and place on kitchen paper to absorb excess oil till cool.

- Flatten each pakoda between your palms.

- Reheat oil and fry pakodé in batches once again till crisp and golden. Drain and place on kitchen paper to absorb excess oil.

- Serve with any chutney of your choice.

PATATAN JA PAKODA
Potato Fritters
Serves: 5

2 medium potatoes, parboiled, peeled and sliced into thin rounds
4 tbsp sai chutney (p. 226)
Oil for deep frying

Pakoda batter:

1 cup gram flour (besan)
A large pinch sodium bicarbonate
¼ tsp salt
1 tsp cumin seeds
2 green chillies, minced
2 tbsp chopped coriander leaves

- Combine all ingredients for batter in a bowl and mix well. Add about ¼ cup water, a little at a time, and mix to make a thick batter of pouring consistency.

- Sandwich 2 slices of potatoes with chutney.

- Heat oil in a kadhai or deep frying pan to smoking point over high heat. Lower heat to moderate, dip potato sandwiches into batter to coat completely. Fry pakodé in batches till golden. Drain and place on kitchen paper to absorb excess oil.

- Serve hot with roti.

Variations: Whole spinach leaves, quartered hardboiled eggs, and thin slices of tomatoes, onions, ashgourd (petha), bottlegourd (lauki) and aubergines (baingan) can be dipped in batter, without sandwiching with chutney, and fried in the same way.

MIRCH JA PAKODA
Chilli Fritters
Serves: 5

100 gms green chillies
¼ tsp red chilli powder
½ tsp mango powder (amchur)
¼ tsp salt
Pakoda batter made with 1 cup gram flour (p. 157)
Oil for deep frying

- Wash chillies and dry thoroughly. Trim heads and make a slit to come halfway down chillies.

- Combine spice powders with salt and stuff into chillies.

- Dip in batter and fry as given for patatan ja pakoda (p. 157).

TEEVAN JA PAKODA
Mutton Fritters
Serves: 5

5 mutton chops
Pakoda batter made with 1 cup gram flour (p. 157)
Oil for deep frying

- Wash chops and pat dry. Trim and beat with a wooden mallet to break fibres. Steam for 30 minutes.

- Dip in batter and fry as given for patatan ja pakoda (p. 157).

SEYAL DABULROTI
Spiced Bread
Serves: 4

8 bread slices
2 tbsp oil

Ground to a fine paste:

1 large onion, roughly chopped
2 medium tomatoes, roughly chopped
½ tsp ginger paste
½ tsp garlic paste
3 tbsp chopped coriander leaves
3 tbsp chopped fenugreek leaves (methi)
8 mint leaves, chopped
8 curry leaves
½ tsp turmeric powder
½ tsp red chilli powder
1 tsp coriander-cumin powder
½ tsp salt

Garnish:

3 tbsp gram flour strings (sev)

- Cut bread slices into ½" cubes.

- Heat oil in a frying pan over low heat. Add ground paste and fry stirring frequently for about 5 minutes till oil rises to the surface.

- Mix in bread. Cook stirring continuously till bread is completely coated with spices.

- Garnish with gram flour strings and serve in individual plates.

PATATAN JOON CHAPIYOON
Potato Cutlets
Serves: 6

6 medium potatoes, boiled, peeled and mashed
6 bread slices, soaked in water and squeezed dry
1 tsp cumin seeds
½ tsp salt
Oil for shallow frying

Filling:

1 cup Bengal gram (chana dal)
½ tsp turmeric powder
¼ tsp salt
2 tbsp blanched, peeled and sliced almonds
2 tbsp blanched, peeled and sliced pistachio nuts
2 tbsp sultanas (kishmish)
2 tbsp chopped coriander leaves
4 green chillies, minced
1 tsp minced ginger
½ tsp red chilli powder
1 tbsp coriander-cumin powder
½ tsp garam masala powder

- Wash dal for filling and soak in water for 1 hour.

- Drain dal and place in a pressure cooker with turmeric, salt and 1½ cups water. Cook under pressure for 5 minutes. Remove from heat and place cooker under running water to reduce pressure immediately. The grains should be tender but separate.

- Cool and combine with remaining ingredients for filling.

- Mix potatoes with bread, cumin and salt and knead to make a smooth dough.

The Essential Sindhi Cookbook

- Divide potato and filling into 10 portions each. Roll each potato portion into a ball and flatten to form a disc. Place a portion of filling in the centre and work potato around filling to cover completely. Shape into heart-shaped cutlets.

- Heat oil in a large frying pan and fry cutlets in batches till light brown on both sides. Drain and place on kitchen paper to absorb excess oil.

- Serve hot with any chutney of your choice.

KHEEMEIN JA SAMOSA
Mince-filled Pastries
Makes: 10 samosé

2 cups + 2 tsp plain flour (maida)
½ tsp salt
½ tsp black cumin seeds (kala jeera)
3 tbsp ghee
Oil for deep frying

Filling:

250 gms minced mutton, boiled
½ cup green peas, boiled
1 medium potato, boiled, peeled and finely diced
1 tsp minced ginger
2 green chillies, minced
2 tbsp chopped coriander leaves
½ tsp red chilli powder
1 tbsp coriander-cumin powder
½ tsp garam masala powder
¼ tsp salt

- Sift 2 cups flour with salt into a bowl. Mix in black cumin. Add ghee and rub into flour.

- Add about ½ cup water, a little at a time, and knead to make a stiff pliable dough.

- Cover dough with a damp cloth and set aside to rest for 15 minutes.

- Mix 2 tsp flour with 2 tbsp water to make a thin paste.

- Mix together all ingredients for filling.

- Knead dough again. Pinch off lime-sized balls of dough. Roll on a floured surface into 6" round roti.

- Cut each roti into half and moisten edges with flour paste. Shape each half into a cone and place 2-3 tbsp of filling inside. Fold top flap down and press to seal.

- Heat oil in a kadhai or deep frying pan over moderate heat and fry samosé in batches till light brown, basting frequently. Drain and place on kitchen paper to absorb excess oil.

- Serve hot with any chutney of your choice.

DAHI BHALLA
Black Bean Fritters in Curd
Serves: 6

1 heaped cup husked black beans (urad dal)
½ tsp salt
1 tsp grated ginger
Oil for deep frying
½ cup sai chutney (p. 226)
½ cup mithi chutney (p. 227)
2 cups curd, whisked

Filling:

2 tbsp blanched, peeled and slivered almonds
2 tbsp blanched, peeled and slivered pistachio nuts
2 tbsp sultanas (kishmish)

Garnish:

½ tsp red chilli powder
1 tbsp roasted cumin seeds, ground
½ tsp garam masala powder
3 tbsp finely chopped coriander leaves

- Wash dal and soak in water for 5 hours. Drain and grind to a medium-coarse paste. It should be slightly grainy.

- Mix in salt and beat with a fork for 5 minutes till fluffy.

- Mix ginger with 2 cups hot water and set aside.

- Mix together ingredients for filling and set aside.

- Place a damp muslin cloth on a steel plate and place 2 tbsp of dal paste on it. Shape into a 3" round disc with the help of the muslin and sprinkle a little filling along one half of disc. Fold over the other half and press gently with moistened fingers, to seal.

- Heat oil in a kadhai or deep frying pan over moderate heat. Carefully place a bhalla into oil and fry till golden. Drain and place in ginger-flavoured hot water for 5 minutes. Squeeze out water from bhalla and place in a serving dish. Repeat with remaining bhallé.

- Sprinkle both chutneys over bhallé and cover with curd. Mix together spice powders for garnish and sprinkle over curd. Garnish with coriander leaves and serve.

CHANA DABULROTI
Chickpeas with Bread
Serves: 6

3 tbsp oil
1 tsp cumin seeds
1 heaped cup chickpeas (Kabuli chana), boiled
1 tbsp red chilli powder
1 tbsp mango powder (amchur)
½ tsp garam masala powder
1 tbsp chola masala (commercially available)
1 tsp crushed pomegranate seeds (anardana)
½ tsp salt
¼ cup sai chutney (p. 226)
8 bread slices

Garnish:

1 medium onion, minced
1 large tomato, finely chopped
4 green chillies, minced
4 tbsp chopped coriander leaves
1 cup gram flour strings (sev)

- Heat oil in a pan over moderate heat. Add cumin seeds and when they stop spluttering, mix in chickpeas, spice powders, pomegranate seeds and salt. Stir and cook for about 5 minutes.

- Mix together onion, tomato, green chillies and coriander leaves for garnish.

- Spread chutney on bread slices, spoon chickpeas over bread and top with onion mixture. Sprinkle with gram flour strings and serve.

Roti and Sindhi Breads

PHULKO
Sindhi Roti
Makes: 6 phulko

2 cups whole-wheat flour (atta)
Ghee for smearing

- Sift flour into a bowl. Add about 1 cup water, a little at a time, and knead to make a stiff, pliable dough.

- Divide dough into 6 portions and roll each portion on a floured surface into a 6" round roti.

- Heat a tava or griddle over moderate heat. Place a roti on tava and roast for about 1 minute till base is dry and brown flecks appear on it. Flip over and roast the other side.

- Remove tava from heat and using tongs, place phulko on a direct flame till it puffs up. (You can also press the phulko while still on the tava with a clean kitchen cloth on all sides using a rotating motion, till it puffs up.)

- Remove from heat, smear with ghee and serve hot.

Variation: **Koki (Sindhi Roti):** Cook the roti on a greased tava or griddle for 2-3 minutes on each side till golden brown. In this case, the roti will not puff up. Serve for breakfast with fried eggs, plain tea or a bowl of seasoned curd.

MASALÉWARI KOKI
Spiced Sindhi Roti
Makes: 5 koki

2 cups whole-wheat flour (atta)
¾ tsp salt
1 medium onion, minced
1 medium tomato, finely chopped
1 tbsp finely chopped green chillies
2 tbsp finely chopped coriander leaves
3 tbsp + 2½ tbsp melted ghee
Butter for smearing koki (optional)

- Sift flour with salt into a bowl. Mix in remaining ingredients except 3 tbsp ghee and butter. Add about ¾ cup water, a little at a time, and knead to make a stiff, pliable dough.

- Divide dough into 5 portions and roll each portion on a floured surface into a 6" round koki.

- Heat ½ tbsp ghee on a tava or griddle over moderate heat. Place a koki on tava and cook for 2-3 minutes on each side till golden brown. Make remaining koki in the same way.

- Smear koki with a little butter (if used) and serve for breakfast with fried eggs, plain tea or a bowl of seasoned curd.

KUTTI
Mashed, Sweet Sindhi Roti
Serves: 3

2 cups whole-wheat flour (atta)
12 tbsp ghee or butter
6 tbsp sugar or grated jaggery

- Sift flour into a bowl. Add about 1 cup water, a little at a time, and knead to make a stiff, pliable dough.

- Divide dough into 6 portions and roll each portion on a floured surface into a 6" round roti.

- Heat a tava or griddle over moderate heat and cook 1 roti at a time for 2-3 minutes on each side till golden brown.

- Place 2 roti in a bowl and while still hot, add 4 tbsp ghee or butter and 2 tbsp sugar or jaggery. Crush and mash roti with your fingers till it becomes a coarse paste, like dry porridge.

- Serve immediately for breakfast with seasoned curd.

LOLO
Jaggery-filled Roti
Makes: 6 lolo

2 cups whole-wheat flour (atta)
1 cup grated jaggery
6 tbsp ghee or butter

- Sift flour into a bowl. Add 1 cup water, a little at a time, and knead to make a stiff, pliable dough.

- Divide dough into 6 portions and roll each portion on a floured surface into a 6" round roti.

- Moisten edges of roti and sprinkle jaggery thickly on one half. Fold other half over jaggery. Press edges with your fingers to seal.

- Heat ½ tbsp ghee or butter on a tava or griddle over moderate heat. Place a lolo on tava and cook for about 2 minutes on each side till golden.

- Transfer lolo to a plate, make tiny gashes on top with a knife, place ½ tbsp ghee or butter on it and serve piping hot for breakfast.

- Make remaining lolo in the same way.

SEYAL MAANI
Spiced Roti
Serves: 2

This dish tastes better if the roti are 1-2 days old.

2 tbsp ghee
1 medium onion, minced
1 tsp grated ginger
1 tsp minced garlic
2 medium tomatoes, diced
2 green chillies, chopped
4 tbsp chopped coriander leaves
6 mint leaves, chopped
6 curry leaves, chopped
¼ tsp turmeric powder
¼ tsp red chilli powder
1 tsp coriander-cumin powder
½ tsp salt
4-6 plain roti, preferably 1-2 days old

- Heat ghee in a frying pan over moderate heat. Add onion, ginger and garlic and fry till onion turns translucent.

- Mix in remaining ingredients except roti. Cook over moderate heat for about 5 minutes till well blended and dry.

- Break roti into small pieces, stir into pan and cook for a few minutes longer.

- Serve hot for breakfast.

DAL JO PHULKO
Lentil-filled Paratha
Makes: 6 phulko

2 cups whole-wheat flour (atta)
¼ tsp salt
6 tsp oil
Butter for smearing

Filling:

1 cup husked green beans (moong dal)
1 small onion, minced
2 green chillies, minced
2 tbsp chopped coriander leaves
1 tbsp mango powder (amchur)
¼ tsp salt

- Wash dal, soak in water for 30 minutes and drain.

- Place dal in a pan with 1½ cups water over moderate heat. Bring to boil, lower heat and cover pan. Simmer for about 15 minutes till grains are tender but remain separate.

- Drain dal thoroughly, mix with remaining ingredients for filling and set aside.

- Sift flour with salt into a bowl. Add about 1 cup water, a little at a time, and knead to make a stiff, pliable dough.

- Divide filling into 6 portions and dough into 12 portions. Roll each portion of dough on a floured surface into a 6" round roti.

- Moisten edges of roti with water. Spread a portion of

filling in the centre of a roti and cover with another roti. Press edges with your fingers to seal.

- Sprinkle some flour on top and gently roll into an 8" round phulko. Make remaining phulko in the same way.

- Heat a tava or griddle over moderate heat and place a phulko on it. Cook for 1 minute till brown spots appear on the base. Gently turn over and cook the other side for 1 minute.

- Dribble ½ tsp oil around edges and cook for 1 minute longer. Turn over, dribble ½ tsp oil around edges and cook for another minute.

- Smear with butter and serve with seasoned curd and mango pickle for breakfast.

MURI JO PHULKO
Radish-filled Paratha
Makes: 6 phulko

2 cups whole-wheat flour (atta)
½ tsp salt
6 tbsp ghee + extra for smearing

Filling:

2 cups finely grated white radish
2 tbsp finely chopped coriander leaves
2 green chillies, minced
1 tsp crushed pomegranate seeds
½ tsp salt

- Sift flour with salt into a bowl. Add about 1 cup water, a little at a time, and knead to make a stiff, pliable dough.

- Squeeze out all water from radish. Mix with remaining ingredients for filling.

- Divide filling into 6 portions and dough into 12 portions. Roll each portion on a floured surface into a 6" round roti.

- Moisten edges of roti with a little water. Spread a portion of filling in the centre of a roti, leaving a ¼" edge and sprinkle with a little flour. Cover with another roti and press edges firmly to seal.

- Press down gently and roll on a floured surface into an 8" round phulko. Make remaining phulko in the same way.

- Heat a tava or griddle over low heat and smear with

½ tbsp ghee. Place a phulko on tava and cook till base is golden. Dribble ½ tbsp ghee around edges of phulko, turn over and cook the other side till golden.

- Smear with extra ghee and serve with seasoned curd.

Variations: **Gul Gobhi jo Phulko (Cauliflower-filled Paratha):** Mix together 1½ cups grated cauliflower, 2 minced green chillies, 2 tbsp chopped coriander leaves, ¼ tsp red chilli powder and ½ tsp salt and use as the filling.

Patatan jo Phulko (Potato-filled Paratha): Mix together 1 cup boiled and mashed potatoes, 2 minced green chillies, 1 small chopped onion, 2 tbsp chopped coriander leaves, 1 tsp mango powder (amchur) and ½ tsp salt and use as the filling.

PAKWAN
Crisp-fried Biscuits
Makes: 4 pakwan

1 cup plain flour (maida)
¼ tsp salt
½ tsp black peppercorns, coarsely ground
½ tsp black cumin seeds (kala jeera)
2 tbsp ghee
Oil for deep frying

- Sift flour with salt into a bowl. Mix in spices and rub in ghee. Add about ½ cup water, a little at a time, and knead to make a stiff, pliable dough.

- Divide dough into 4 portions and roll each portion on a floured surface into a 6" round biscuit. Prick biscuits all over with a fork to prevent them from puffing up while frying.

- Heat oil in a kadhai or deep frying pan over moderate heat and fry 1 pakwan at a time till crisp and golden. Drain and place on kitchen paper to absorb excess oil.

- Serve with khatti dal (p. 130).

POORI
Deep-fried Bread
Makes: 10 poori

2 cups whole-wheat flour (atta)
½ tsp salt
1 tbsp ghee
Oil for deep frying

- Sift flour with salt into a bowl. Add ghee and rub into flour. Add about 1 cup water, a little at a time, and knead to make a stiff, pliable dough.

- Divide dough into 10 portions and roll each portion on a floured surface into a 4" round poori.

- Heat oil in a frying pan to smoking point over high heat. Lower heat to moderate and fry 1 poori at a time. Press with a spatula so that it puffs up. Turn and fry the other side till golden.

- Poori are normally served with makhani dal (p. 133), sooji jo halwo (p. 199) or aam rus (mango pulp).

CHEHRI POORI
Spicy Deep-fried Bread
Makes: 10 poori

2 cups whole-wheat flour (atta)
½ tsp salt
1 tbsp ghee
½ tsp turmeric powder
2 tbsp chopped coriander leaves
4 green chillies, minced
1 small onion, minced
Oil for deep frying

- Sift flour with salt into a bowl. Add ghee and rub into flour. Mix in remaining ingredients except oil. Add about 1 cup water, a little at a time, and knead to make a stiff, pliable dough.

- Divide dough into 10 portions and roll each portion on a floured surface into a 4" round poori.

- Heat ghee in a frying pan to smoking point over high heat. Lower heat to moderate and fry 1 poori at a time. Press with a spatula so that it puffs up. Turn and fry the other side till golden.

- Serve with seasoned curd.

CHILO
Sindhi Pancakes
Makes: 10 chilo

2 cups gram flour (besan)
½ tsp salt
½ tsp turmeric powder
1 small onion, minced
2 tsp minced ginger
1 large tomato, finely chopped
2 green chillies, minced
3 tbsp finely chopped coriander leaves
7 tbsp ghee

- Mix together all ingredients except ghee in a bowl. Add ¾ cup water, a little at a time, and mix to make a thick batter of pouring consistency.

- Heat a non-stick frying pan over low heat and smear with 1 tsp ghee. Pour in 2 tbsp of batter. Spread to form a 5" round chilo. Cook for 3-4 minutes till base is golden. Dribble 1 tsp ghee around edges, flip over and cook for 3-4 minutes longer, till the other side is golden.

- Serve immediately with any chutney of your choice.

JOWAR JO DHODHO
Milo Flour Roti
Makes: 6 dhodho

2 cups milo flour (jowar ka atta)
½ tsp salt
12 tbsp ghee
6 tbsp butter

Ground to a coarse paste:
4 tbsp chopped coriander leaves
4 tbsp chopped green garlic or 1 tsp chopped garlic
8 mint leaves, chopped
1 small onion, roughly chopped
2 green chillies, roughly chopped

- Sift flour with salt into a bowl. Mix in ground paste. Add 1 cup water, a little at a time, and knead to make a stiff dough.

- Divide dough into 6 portions and roll each portion on a floured surface into a thick, 5" round roti.

- Heat a tava or griddle over low heat and smear with 1 tbsp ghee. Place a roti on tava and cook till base is golden. Dribble 1 tbsp ghee around edges of roti, flip over and cook the other side till golden.

- Smear with 1 tbsp butter and serve hot with panchratni dal (p. 134), tridali (p. 136) or any mutton dish.

MITHI KOKI
Sweet Roti
Makes: 4 koki

Mithi koki are especially made for the festival of Thadree.

2 cups whole-wheat flour (atta)
5 tbsp + 4 tsp melted ghee
6 tbsp grated jaggery

- Sift flour into a bowl and rub in 5 tbsp ghee.

- Place jaggery in a pan with ½ cup water over moderate heat and stir till jaggery dissolves.

- Strain jaggery into flour and knead to make a stiff dough. If the dough is not stiff add more flour. Cover dough with a damp cloth and set aside to rest for 15 minutes.

- Knead dough again. Divide into 4 portions and roll each portion on a floured surface into a thick, 5" round roti.

- Heat a tava or griddle over low heat and smear with ½ tsp ghee. Place a roti on tava and cook till base is golden. Dribble ½ tsp ghee around edges of roti, flip over and cook the other side till golden.

- These koki are eaten with mango pickle. They can last for a week in an airtight container.

BESAN JI KOKI
Gram Flour Roti
Makes: 6 koki

These are made for the festival of Thadree.

3 cups gram flour (besan)
¾ tsp salt
4 tbsp + 6 tbsp melted ghee
1 tbsp crushed pomegranate seeds
1 small onion, minced
3 green chillies, minced
2 tbsp finely chopped coriander leaves

- Sift flour with salt into a bowl. Add 4 tbsp ghee and rub into flour. Mix in remaining ingredients except 6 tbsp ghee. Add about ½ cup water, a little at a time, and knead to make a stiff, pliable dough.

- Divide dough into 6 portions and roll each portion on a floured surface into a 5" round roti.

- Heat a tava or griddle over low heat and smear with ½ tbsp ghee. Place a roti on tava and cook till base is golden. Dribble ½ tbsp ghee around edges of roti, flip over and cook the other side till golden.

- These koki can last for a week in an airtight container.

CUSTOMER SALE   0153/0008/6705-4
3266 JORNA   15-FEB-06 10:22

** CUSTOMER COPY **
80/71 TOTAL TABLE TOP
225009 1@ 1.99   1.99

    1 ITEMS SUBTOTAL   1.99

         TOTAL   1.99

         CASH   2.00

         CHANGE   0.01

TK Maxx
Registered Office: 50 Clarendon Road, Watford, WD17 1TX
VAT Reg. 662 5635 24

www.tkmaxx.com

Thank you for shopping with us. See you again soon.

Happy with your purchase? If not, TK Maxx is pleased to offer a
refund or exchange on any item returned in its original condition and
packaging, together with the receipt within 30 days. Please note there
is a 10 working day delay for refunds on purchases made by cheque.
Your statutory rights are not affected.

Job Opportunities

KHAKHAD
Crisp-fried Sweet Biscuits
Makes: 8 khakhad

These are also made for the festival of Thadree.

2 cups plain flour (maida)
½ cup castor sugar
3 tbsp melted ghee
Oil for deep frying

- Sift flour into a bowl and mix in sugar. Add ghee and rub into flour. Add about 1 cup water, a little at a time, and knead to make a stiff dough. Set aside to rest for 30 minutes.

- Knead dough again and divide into 8 portions. Roll each portion on a floured surface into a thin, 8" round khakhad. Prick all over with a fork to prevent them from puffing up while frying.

- Heat oil in a kadhai or deep frying pan and fry 1 khakhad at a time till crisp and golden. Drain and place on kitchen paper to absorb excess oil.

- Cool completely and store in an airtight container. Khakhad will last for a week.

TIKKI
Sweet Biscuits with Nuts
Makes: 5 tikki

Tikki are especially made for the festival of Thadree.

2 cups plain flour (maida)
½ cup castor sugar
4 tbsp ghee
Oil for deep frying

Topping:

3 tbsp castor sugar
1 tbsp powdered green cardamom
3 tbsp blanched, peeled and ground almonds
3 tbsp blanched, peeled and ground pistachio nuts

- Sift flour into a bowl and mix in sugar. Add ghee and rub into flour. Add about ¾ cup water, a little at a time, and knead to make a stiff dough. Set aside to rest for 30 minutes.

- Knead dough again and divide into 5 portions. Roll each portion on a floured surface into a thick, 5" round biscuit. Prick all over with a fork to prevent them from puffing up while frying. Cut each biscuit into quarters.

- Heat oil in a kadhai or deep frying pan and fry tikki in batches till golden. Drain and place on kitchen paper to absorb excess oil.

- Mix sugar with cardamom powder and sprinkle over tikki. Sprinkle ground nuts over this and serve.

Sweets and Desserts

MAZOON
Mixed Nut Sweet
Makes: 25 sweets

½ cup walnuts
½ cup almonds, blanched and peeled
½ cup cashewnuts
½ cup pistachio nuts, blanched and peeled
4 cups sugar
500 gms khoya, crumbled (p. 233)
2 tbsp poppy seeds (khus-khus)
1 tbsp coarsely ground green cardamom seeds

Decoration:

5-6 sheets silver leaf (chandi ka varq)

- Grind nuts coarsely and set aside.

- Place sugar in a pan with 2 cups water over moderate heat and stir till sugar dissolves. Raise heat and bring to boil. Continue boiling till syrup reaches the thread stage. (A little syrup poured into a cup of cold water will form a thin thread.)

- Lower heat to moderate and mix in nuts, khoya, poppy seeds and cardamom. Cook stirring continuously till mixture leaves sides of pan.

- Remove from heat and transfer to a greased tray. Spread to make a ½" thick layer. Level surface with greased hands and decorate with silver leaf.

- Allow to cool and cut into 1" diamonds.

- Store in an airtight container.

BADAMIYOON JI MITHAI
Almond Sweet
Makes: 15 sweets

2 cups sugar
250 gms khoya, crumbled (p. 233)
250 gms almonds, blanched, peeled and ground
1 tsp coarsely ground green cardamom seeds
A few drops almond essence

Decoration:
2 tbsp blanched, peeled and shredded almonds

- Place sugar in a pan with 1 cup water over moderate heat and stir till sugar dissolves. Raise heat and bring to boil. Continue boiling till syrup is thick.

- Reduce heat to low and mix in khoya, almonds and cardamom. Cook stirring continuously till mixture leaves sides of pan.

- Remove from heat, mix in essence and transfer to a greased tray. Spread to make a ½" thick layer. Level surface with greased hands and decorate with shredded almonds.

- Allow to cool and cut into 1" diamonds.

- Store in an airtight container.

Variation: **Khajun ji Mithai (Cashewnut Sweet):** Use cashewnuts in place of almonds. Omit essence and decorate with silver leaf.

Pistan ji Mithai (Pistachio nut sweet): Use pistachio nuts in place of almonds. Omit essence, add a few drops of green food colour if you like and decorate with silver leaf.

BESAN JI MITHAI
Gram Flour Sweet
Makes: 16 sweets

½ cup ghee
2 cups gram flour (besan)
2¼ cups castor sugar
1 tsp powdered green cardamom seeds
2 tbsp blanched, peeled and sliced almonds
2 tbsp blanched, peeled and sliced pistachio nuts

Decoration:
2 tbsp blanched, peeled and sliced almonds
2 tbsp blanched, peeled and sliced pistachio nuts

- Heat ghee in a large pan over low heat. Add gram flour and fry stirring continuously till golden.

- Remove from heat, mix in remaining ingredients except nuts for decoration and transfer to a greased tray. Spread to make a ½" thick layer. Level surface with greased hands and decorate with nuts.

- Allow to cool and cut into 1" diamonds.

- Store in an airtight container.

SINGAR JI MITHAI
Gram Flour String Sweet
Makes: about 30 sweets

4½ cups sugar
500 gms khoya, crumbled (p. 233)
500 gms salt-free fine gram flour strings (sev)
1 tbsp coarsely ground green cardamom seeds
A few drops rose essence

Decoration:
3 tbsp blanched, peeled and sliced almonds
3 tbsp blanched, peeled and sliced pistachio nuts
5-6 sheets silver leaf (chandi ka varq)

- Place sugar in a pan with 1½ cups water over moderate heat and stir till sugar dissolves. Raise heat and bring to boil. Continue boiling till syrup reaches the thread stage. (A little syrup poured into a cup of cold water will form a thin thread.)

- Reduce heat to low and mix in khoya, gram flour strings and cardamom. Cook stirring continuously till mixture leaves sides of pan.

- Remove from heat, mix in essence and transfer to a greased tray. Spread to make a ½" thick layer. Level surface with greased hands and decorate with nuts and silver leaf.

- Allow to cool and cut into 1" diamonds.

- Store in an airtight container.

NAREL JI MITHAI
Coconut Sweet
Makes: 12 sweets

4 tbsp ghee
2 cups finely grated fresh coconut
2 cups sugar
1 cup crumbled khoya (p. 233)
1 tsp green cardamom seeds, coarsely ground
2 tbsp blanched, peeled and sliced almonds
2 tbsp blanched, peeled and sliced pistachio nuts
A few drops rose essence

Decoration:

3-4 sheets silver leaf (chandi ka várq)

- Heat ghee in a large pan over low heat. Add coconut and fry till brown, stirring continuously. Add sugar and continue to stir till sugar melts.

- Mix in khoya and cardamom and keep on stirring till mixture leaves sides of pan.

- Remove from heat, stir in nuts and essence and transfer to a greased tray. Spread to make a ½" thick layer. Level surface with greased hands and decorate with silver leaf.

- Allow to cool and cut into 1" diamonds.

- Store in an airtight container.

TIRRAN JA LADOO
Sesame Seed Sweet
Makes: about 30 ladoo

These ladoo are especially served during the festival of Tirmoori.

500 gms white sesame seeds (til)
4 tbsp ghee
4½ cups castor sugar
2 tbsp blanched, peeled and sliced almonds
2 tbsp blanched, peeled and sliced pistachio nuts
2 tbsp sultanas (kishmish)
1 tbsp green cardamom seeds

- Heat a tava or griddle over moderate heat. Add sesame seeds and roast stirring continuously till light brown. Transfer to a bowl and set aside.

- Heat ghee in a large pan over moderate heat. Add sugar and stir till it melts.

- Mix in remaining ingredients and keep on stirring till mixture thickens and leaves sides of pan.

- While mixture is still hot, but cool enough to handle, dip your hands in water, pinch off lime-sized balls and shape into round ladoo.

- Place on a metal tray for about 5-6 hours till cool, dry and hard and store in an airtight container.

MALPURO

Rich Pancakes
Makes: about 6 malpuro

1 cup milk
½ cup castor sugar
½ cup whole-wheat flour (atta)
1 tsp aniseed (saunf)
1 tbsp poppy seeds (khus-khus)
1 tsp green cardamom seeds
Ghee for deep frying

- Mix milk and sugar together in a bowl. Add flour, a little at a time, and mix to make a batter of thick pouring consistency. Beat with an egg beater till smooth and thick. Mix in remaining ingredients except ghee.

- Heat ghee in a frying pan to smoking point over high heat. Reduce heat to low and put in 2 tbsp batter. Spread with the back of a ladle into an 8" round malpuro. Fry till base is golden. Flip over and fry the other side till golden.

- Serve hot.

FALOODO KULFI
Kulfi with Cornflour Vermicelli and Thickened Milk
Serves: 10

Rabdi:

1 litre milk
1 cup sugar

Kulfi:

2 tbsp cornflour
2 litres milk
2¼ cups sugar
4 tbsp blanched, peeled, slivered and roasted pistachio nuts
4 tbsp blanched, peeled, slivered and roasted almonds
2 tbsp blanched, peeled, coarsely chopped and roasted almonds
2 tbsp coarsely chopped and roasted cashewnuts
½ tsp saffron strands soaked in 1 tbsp hot milk

Falooda:

250 gms falooda (commercially available)

To serve:

10 tbsp rose syrup
10-12 ice cubes, crushed

Rabdi:

- Place milk and sugar in a large pan over moderate heat and stir till sugar dissolves. Bring to boil and lower heat. Cook over low heat stirring continuously till milk is reduced to a quarter of its original volume.

- Remove from heat, cool and chill in the refrigerator till required.

Kulfi:

- Blend cornflour with ¼ cup of the measured milk and set aside.

- Place sugar with remaining milk in a large pan over moderate heat and stir till sugar dissolves. Bring to boil and lower heat. Cook over low heat till milk is reduced to half its original volume.

- Stir in reserved cornflour and milk paste and cook till it thickens slightly.

- Remove from heat and mix in nuts and saffron. Cool and pour into individual kulfi moulds. Freeze for 8 hours.

Falooda:

- Place a large pan with plenty of water over high heat and bring to boil. Add falooda and boil for about 10 minutes, till tender.

- Pour contents of pan into a strainer and rinse under running cold water. Shake strainer thoroughly to remove excess water.

To serve:

- Place falooda in individual dessert bowls, slice kulfi and place on top of falooda. Pour 1 tbsp of rabdi and rose syrup over kulfi. Top with crushed ice and serve.

MAWÉ JA SAMOSA
Khoya-filled Pastries
Makes: about 8 samosé

This is served during the festival of Holi with gheear.

2 cups plain flour (maida)
3 tbsp ghee
Oil for deep frying

Filling:

1 cup crumbled khoya (p. 233)
2 tbsp blanched, peeled and sliced almonds
2 tbsp blanched, peeled and sliced pistachio nuts
1 tbsp sultanas (kishmish)
1 tsp green cardamom seeds
½ cup castor sugar

- Place flour in a bowl and rub in ghee. Add ¾ cup water, a little at a time, and knead to make a stiff dough. Cover with a damp cloth and set aside for 15 minutes.

- Combine ingredients for filling and mix well.

- Knead dough again. Divide into 16 portions. Roll each portion on a floured surface into a 4" round roti. Moisten edges of roti with a little water.

- Place 2 tbsp filling in the centre of a roti and cover with another roti. Press edges together to seal, and crimp them. Make all samosé in the same way.

- Heat oil in a kadhai or deep frying pan over moderate heat. Fry 1 samosa at a time till golden. Drain and place on kitchen paper to absorb excess oil.

SOOJI JO HALWO
Semolina Halva
Serves: 6

¼ cup ghee
1 cup semolina (sooji/rava)
1 tsp powdered green cardamom
½ cup sugar
¼ tsp saffron strands soaked in 2 tbsp hot milk

Decoration:

2 tbsp blanched, peeled and sliced almonds
2 tbsp blanched, peeled and sliced pistachio nuts

- Heat ghee in a frying pan over low heat. Add semolina and cardamom and fry stirring continuously till semolina turns light brown.

- Stir in sugar and 3 cups hot water. Cook stirring continuously till mixture is dry and ghee rises to the surface.

- Remove from heat, mix in saffron and decorate with nuts.

- Serve hot with plain poori (p. 179).

GHEEAR
Crisp-fried Sweet
Makes: 14-15 gheer

These are usually made during the festival of Holi.

3 cups + 1 cup plain flour (maida)
1 cup curd, whisked
A few drops orange food colour (optional)
3 cups sugar
1 tsp rose essence
Ghee for deep frying

Decoration:
¼ cup blanched, peeled and shredded pistachio nuts

- Mix 3 cups flour with curd in a bowl. Add about 2 cups water, a little at a time, and mix to make a batter of thick pouring consistency. Cover and set aside overnight.

- Mix in 1 cup flour and food colour (if used) and set aside.

- Place sugar in a pan with 1 cup water over moderate heat and stir till sugar dissolves. Raise heat and bring to boil. Continue boiling till syrup thickens. Remove from heat, mix in rose essence and set aside.

- Heat ghee in a kadhai or deep frying pan to smoking point over high heat. Reduce heat to low.

- Fill a small funnel with batter, covering the outlet of the funnel with your finger. Hold funnel over ghee, release your finger and pour batter into hot ghee in concentric circles to form an 8" round disc. Fry over low heat till firm and crisp, taking care not to let it brown.

- Drain and place in sugar syrup for about 4 minutes. Remove from syrup and place in a serving dish. Repeat till batter is used up.

- Decorate with nuts and serve immediately. They lose their crispness very quickly.

Note: Use food colour from a recognized and reputed brand.

BOONDI JI KHIRNI
Milk Pudding with Sweet Gram Flour Balls
Serves: 6

500 ml + 500 ml milk
6 tbsp + 6 tbsp sugar
1 tsp powdered green cardamom
1 cup sweet boondi (commercially available)
¼ cup powdered cashewnuts

Decoration:
2 tbsp blanched, peeled and sliced almonds
2 tbsp blanched, peeled and sliced pistachio nuts

- Place 500 ml milk with 6 tbsp sugar and cardamom in a wide-mouthed pan and boil till thick and creamy. Mix in boondi and set aside.

- Place 500 ml milk with 6 tbsp sugar and cashewnuts in another wide-mouthed pan and boil till it has the consistency of a thick custard.

- Pour into boondi-milk and mix well. Cool and chill in the refrigerator.

- Decorate with nuts and serve chilled.

KHIRNI
Rice Pudding
Serves: 6

This is eaten during the festival of Teejri. The women break their fast with khirni.

¼ cup ghee
¾ cup long-grained rice
1 litre milk
½ cup sugar
1 tbsp powdered green cardamom
¼ tsp saffron strands soaked in 1 tbsp hot milk

Decoration:

2 tbsp blanched, peeled and sliced almonds
2 tbsp blanched, peeled and sliced pistachio nuts

- Heat ghee in a frying pan over low heat. Add rice and fry stirring continuously till golden. Cool and grind to a paste with about 1 tbsp water.

- Place rice paste in a pan with milk, sugar and cardamom. Cook over moderate heat stirring frequently till it has the consistency of a thick custard.

- Remove from heat and mix in saffron. Cool and place in the refrigerator till chilled.

- Decorate with nuts and serve chilled.

CHURI
Jaggery Dessert
Serves: 20

Traditionally, this dessert is made in honour of Lord Shiva, during the festival of Shivratri.

1 cup ghee
1 kg whole-wheat flour (atta)
500 gms grated jaggery
Ghee for deep frying

- Place flour in a bowl and rub in ghee. Add about 2 cups water, a little at a time, and knead to make a stiff dough. Cover with a damp cloth and set aside for 15 minutes.

- Knead dough again. Pinch off lime-sized balls of dough and shape into round ladoo.

- Heat ghee in a kadhai or deep frying pan over moderate heat. Add ladoo and fry in batches till crisp and golden. Drain and place on kitchen paper to absorb excess ghee till cool.

- Place jaggery in a pan with 2 cups water over low heat. Cook stirring occasionally till jaggery dissolves. Strain into a fresh pan and place over high heat. Cook stirring occasionally till it thickens.

- Remove from heat and allow to cool. Coarsely pound ladoo and mix into jaggery syrup.

- This sweet will stay for a few days.

Papad and Kheecha

PAPAD
Makes: 2 kg papad

It is customary to welcome any visitor to a Sindhi house with papad and water.

2 tbsp sodium bicarbonate
2 tbsp salt
1 kg powdered husked black beans (urad dal)
½ kg powdered pigeon peas (arhar/toover)
½ kg powdered husked green beans (moong dal)
3 tbsp black peppercorns, coarsely ground
3 tbsp cumin seeds, coarsely ground
5 tbsp mustard oil

- Place 2½ cups water in a pan over moderate heat. Add sodium bicarbonate and salt and stir till dissolved. Strain through a muslin cloth.

- Blend together all powdered dals and set aside 1 cup.

- Mix remaining powdered dals with pepper and cumin. Add soda water, a little at a time, and knead to make a stiff dough. Cover and set aside overnight.

- Knead dough till smooth and pliable. Pinch off lime-sized balls of dough and dip in mustard oil. Flatten into small discs, dip in reserved powdered dals and roll on a floured surface into paper-thin, 8" round papad.

- Arrange papad on steel trays, cover with fine muslin and place in the sun for 2-3 days till dry and crisp.

- Store in airtight containers.

- To serve, roast over an open flame or deep fry till golden.

KHEECHA
Rice Savoury
Makes: 1 kg kheecha

3 tbsp sodium bicarbonate
3 tbsp salt
2 tbsp cumin seeds, coarsely ground
2 tbsp coarsely ground dry red chillies
1 kg rice flour + extra flour for rolling

- Place 3 litres water in a pan over moderate heat. Add sodium bicarbonate and salt and stir till dissolved. Strain through a muslin cloth into a fresh pan.

- Place pan over moderate heat and add spice powders and rice flour. Cook stirring continuously till it forms a thick, dry dough that leaves sides of pan.

- Remove from heat and place dough on a steel plate. When just cool enough to handle, knead and punch dough till smooth and pliable.

- Pinch off lime-sized balls of dough. Roll each ball on a floured surface into a paper-thin, 8" round kheecha.

- Arrange kheecha on steel trays, cover with fine muslin and place in the sun for 2-3 days till dry and crisp.

- Store in airtight containers.

- To serve, deep fry till crisp and light golden.

PATATAN JOON KACHRIYOON
Potato Wafers
Makes: about 1 kg potato wafers

1 kg new potatoes
¼ tsp salt

- Scrub potatoes thoroughly with a brush and wash well. Keep unpeeled and slice into paper-thin wafers.

- Place potatoes in a pan with salt and water to cover over high heat. Bring to boil and remove from heat.

- Drain potatoes and spread on a plastic sheet. Cover with fine muslin and place in the sun for 1-2 days till dry and crisp.

- Store in airtight containers.

- To serve, deep fry till crisp and light golden.

SABUDANÉ JOON KACHRIYOON

Sago Savouries
Makes: ¼ kg kachriyoon

2 cups sago (sabudana)
1 tsp salt
1 tsp cumin seeds
2 tbsp red chilli powder

- Wash sago well in several changes of water and drain.

- Place 3 cups water in a large pan over high heat and bring to boil. Reduce heat to low and add all ingredients.

- Cook over low heat stirring continuously till it forms a thick, dry dough that leaves sides of pan. Remove from heat and allow to cool.

- Drop tablespoons of mixture on a plastic sheet and shape into 3" round discs. Cover with fine muslin and place in the sun for 1-2 days, till dry and crisp.

- Store in airtight containers.

- To serve, deep fry over low heat till crisp and light golden.

Sherbets

CHANDAN JO SHARBAT
Sandalwood Sherbet
Makes: 750 ml

6¾ cups sugar
30 gms sandalwood powder
2 cups newly opened petals of rose and kewda flowers
6-8 drops yellow food colour (optional)
6-8 sheets silver leaf (chandi ka varq)

- Place sugar in a pan with 1 litre water over low heat and stir till sugar dissolves. Continue cooking over low heat stirring occasionally till syrup is reduced to three-quarters of its original volume.

- Tie sandalwood powder in a piece of muslin cloth and add to pan. Simmer for 2 minutes, remove from heat and set aside to cool.

- Stir in flower petals and food colour (if used). Cover pan and set aside overnight.

- Squeeze out all the juice from the sandalwood bag and discard bag. Strain syrup through a muslin cloth into a jug.

- Chop silver leaf while it is still attached to its backing paper and carefully add to jug. Pour into a clean, sterilized bottle. Close bottle tightly and place in the refrigerator. It will stay for about 1 year.

- To serve, pour about 2 tbsp syrup into a glass and fill with chilled water or soda.

Note: Use food colour from a recognized and reputed brand.

GULAB JO SHARBAT
Rose Sherbet
Makes: 750 ml

6¾ cups sugar
10 green cardamoms, powdered
6-8 drops red food colour (optional)
2 tsp rose essence

- Place sugar in a pan with 1 litre water over low heat and stir till sugar dissolves. Continue cooking over low heat stirring occasionally till syrup is reduced to three-quarters of its original volume.

- Add cardamoms and cook for 5 minutes longer. Remove from heat and add food colour (if used) and essence.

- Pour into clean, sterilized bottles, close tightly and keep in a cool dry place. It will stay for 1 year in the refrigerator.

- To serve, pour about 2 tbsp syrup into a glass and fill with chilled water or milk. Add a scoop of vanilla ice cream for added flavour.

Note: Use food colour from a recognized and reputed brand.

LIMUN JO SHARBAT
Lime Sherbet
Makes: 700 ml

Juice from 24 limes
Sugar equal to volume of lime juice

- Strain lime juice and measure. Stir in an equal volume of sugar.

- Pour into clean, sterilized bottles and close tightly.

- Place in the sun for 1 month, shaking the bottles periodically. At the end of the month the sugar will have dissolved and the syrup will be ready for use.

- This syrup will stay for 1 year.

- To serve, pour 2 tbsp of syrup into a glass and fill with iced water or soda.

THADAL
Mixed Nuts and Milk Drink
Serves: 6

Thadal is specially made during the festivals of Shivratri and Holi. Sometimes a little bhang (fresh cannabis) is added.

1 litre milk
4 tbsp rose syrup

Ground to a paste:
12 almonds, blanched and peeled
12 pistachio nuts, blanched and peeled
12 cashewnuts
1 tsp mixed, powdered green cardamoms, nutmeg and
aniseed (saunf)
½ cup sugar

Decoration:
6 tbsp cream, lightly whipped
A few fresh red rose petals

- Place milk, rose syrup and ground paste in a blender and blend till smooth.

- Strain and chill.

- To serve, pour thadal into glasses, swirl 1 tbsp cream into each glass and decorate with rose petals.

MATTHO
Curd Cocktail
Serves: 6

This drink is served during the Thadree festival only.

2½ cups curd, whisked
4 tbsp castor sugar
¼ tsp black pepper powder
2 tsp ground mustard seeds
½ tsp salt
2 tbsp finely chopped coriander leaves
1 cup gram flour strings (sev)
2 tbsp blanched, peeled and sliced pistachio nuts
2 tbsp sultanas (kishmish)

- Combine curd, sugar, spice powders, salt and 3 cups water in a blender and blend till smooth.
- Mix in remaining ingredients and place in the refrigerator for at least 30 minutes.
- Serve chilled.

Pickles, Chutneys and Preserves

KHATTI MITHI AMBRIYOON JI KHATAIN
Sweet and Sour Mango Pickle
Makes: 3½ kg

2½ kg medium tender, unripe mangoes
4" stick cinnamon, broken
10 cloves
4 tbsp cumin seeds
4 bay leaves (tej patta), crushed
4 tbsp salt
1 kg jaggery, grated
2½ cups white vinegar

- Wash mangoes and dry thoroughly.

- Cut mangoes into quarters. Remove and discard seeds. Spread on a steel tray, sprinkle with spices and salt and set aside for 2-3 hours.

- Place jaggery and vinegar in a pan over moderate heat. Cook stirring occasionally till jaggery dissolves. Strain jaggery syrup through a muslin cloth into a fresh pan.

- Cool syrup and mix into mangoes. Place in clean, sterilized, airtight jars.

- Cover tightly and tie mouth of jars with muslin cloth. Place in the sun for about 2 weeks.

- This pickle will stay for 1 year.

AMBRIYOON JI KHATAIN
Mango Pickle
Makes: about 1 kg

1 kg unripe tender mangoes
250 gms salt
4 tbsp turmeric powder
1¼ cups mustard oil + extra as needed
½ cup husked fenugreek seeds (methi dal)
½ cup husked mustard seeds
½ tsp asafoetida powder (hing)
¼ cup red chilli powder

- Wash mangoes and dry thoroughly. Cut into 1" pieces. Remove and discard seeds.

- Mix salt and turmeric together and mix into mangoes. Set aside overnight.

- Drain out water from mangoes and pour into a pan. Place pan over high heat and bring to boil. Remove from heat and allow to cool.

- Place oil in another pan over high heat till it reaches smoking point. Remove from heat and allow to cool.

- Mix reserved mango water with oil and remaining spices. Mix in mangoes and place in clean, sterilized, airtight jars. Cover tightly and keep in the sun for 2 weeks.

- Check regularly that oil covers mangoes completely. If not, heat some more oil to smoking point, cool and pour over mangoes to cover completely.

- This pickle will stay for 1 year.

BASARAN JI KHATAIN
Onion Pickle
Makes: 500 gms

500 gms baby onions, peeled
1 cup mustard oil
2 tbsp red chilli powder
3 tbsp ground mustard seeds
2 tbsp turmeric powder
3 tbsp salt

- Mix together all ingredients and place in a clean, sterilized, airtight jar. Place in the sun for 2 days.

- This pickle will stay for about 2 weeks.

Variations: Use turnips, carrots or white radish, scraped and cut into 2" strips instead of onions.

KANJI
Carrot Pickle
Makes: 250 gms

250 gms carrots
2 tbsp ground mustard seeds
2 tbsp red chilli powder
2 tbsp salt
1 small beetroot, peeled and chopped

- Wash carrots and dry thoroughly. Peel and cut lengthwise into 6-8 pieces each.

- Combine spices and beetroot with 2½ cups boiled, cooled water in a bowl. Place carrots in a clean sterilized, airtight jar and pour spiced water over them. Place in the sun for 2 days.

- This pickle will stay for 3-4 days only.

Note: The water from this pickle makes a very good appetizer when served chilled.

LIMUN JI KHATAIN
Lime Pickle
Makes: 2 kg

30 thin-skinned limes
250 gms ginger, julienned
250 gms thick green chillies, slit but kept whole
250 gms sea salt

- Wash limes and dry thoroughly.

- Cut half the limes into 4 pieces each and remove and discard seeds. Extract juice from remaining limes.

- Mix all ingredients together and place in a clean, sterilized, airtight jar. Place in the sun for 2-3 days.

- This pickle will stay for 1 year.

GIDAMBRI JI CHUTNEY
Tamarind Chutney
Makes: 2 cups

6 pods green tamarind, peeled and seeded
1 cup chopped coriander leaves, tightly packed
½ cup chopped mint leaves, tightly packed
4 green chillies, roughly chopped
1 medium onion, roughly chopped
½ tsp salt

- Grind all ingredients together to a smooth paste.
- Store in the refrigerator for up to 2 days.

SAI CHUTNEY
Green Chutney
Makes: 2 cups

1 cup chopped mint leaves, tightly packed
½ cup chopped coriander leaves, tightly packed
1 small unripe mango, peeled and roughly chopped
1 small onion, roughly chopped
2 green chillies, roughly chopped
1 tbsp minced ginger
1 tsp cumin seeds
2 tbsp sugar
Juice of 1 lime
½ tsp salt

- Grind all ingredients together to a smooth paste.

- Store in the refrigerator for up to 2 days.

PHUDINA JI CHUTNEY
Mint Chutney
Makes: about 3 cups

2 cups chopped mint leaves, tightly packed
1 cup chopped coriander leaves, tightly packed
4 green chillies, roughly chopped
1 medium onion, roughly chopped
1 tbsp grated ginger
Juice of 1 large lime
1 tsp salt

- Grind all ingredients together to a smooth paste.

- Store in the refrigerator for up to 2 days.

DHAROON JI CHUTNEY
Fresh Pomegranate Seed Chutney
Makes: 1 cup

1 cup fresh pomegranate seeds
¼ cup chopped mint leaves, tightly packed
¼ cup chopped coriander leaves, tightly packed
2 green chillies, roughly chopped
1 tsp grated ginger
½ tsp salt

- Grind all ingredients together to a smooth paste.
- Store in the refrigerator for up to 2 days.

MITHI CHUTNEY
Sweet Chutney
Makes: 1 ½ cups

6 dates, seeded
6 tbsp thick tamarind juice
1 tsp black salt (kala namak)
1 tsp cumin seeds, ground
½ tsp garam masala powder
1 tbsp grated ginger
½ cup grated jaggery
½ tsp salt

- Grind all ingredients together to a smooth paste.
- Store in the refrigerator for up to 2 days.

AMB JO MURRABO
Mango Preserve
Makes: 2 kg

12 semi-ripe alphonso mangoes
1½ kg sugar
½ tsp salt
4 tbsp blanched, peeled and sliced almonds
4 tbsp blanched, peeled and sliced pistachio nuts
1 tbsp green cardamom seeds
½ tsp saffron strands soaked in 1 tbsp hot water

- Peel mangoes and slice flesh.

- Place sugar in a pan with 6 cups water over moderate heat and stir till sugar dissolves.

- Lower heat, add mangoes and salt. Cook over low heat stirring frequently till mangoes are soft and translucent.

- Remove from heat and mix in remaining ingredients.

- Cool and place in clean, sterilized, airtight jars.

- This preserve will stay for 2 years in the refrigerator or 3 months outside.

GAJROON JO MURRABO

Carrot Preserve
Makes: 1½ kg

1 kg red carrots
1 kg sugar
1 tbsp green cardamom seeds
½ tsp saffron strands soaked in 2 tbsp water
1 tsp citric acid (nimbu ka phool)
5-6 sheets silver leaf (chandi ka varq)

- Scrape carrots and cut lengthwise into thick slices. Pierce them all over with a skewer or fork.

- Place carrots in a pan with water to cover over high heat and bring to boil. Reduce heat to low and cook for about 15 minutes till almost tender. Drain and spread on a kitchen cloth for 2 hours till dry.

- Place sugar in a pan with 5 cups water over moderate heat and stir till sugar dissolves.

- Reduce heat to low and add carrots. Cook over low heat for 20-25 minutes till syrup thickens. Remove from heat and mix in cardamom, saffron and citric acid.

- Cool and place in a clean, sterilized, airtight jar. Chop silver leaf while it is still attached to its backing paper and carefully add to jar.

- This preserve will stay for 1 year in the refrigerator or 3 months outside.

Glossary

English	Hindi	Sindhi
Almonds	Badam	Badamiyoon
Aniseed	Saunf	Saunf
Apple	Seb	Soof
Asafoetida	Hing	Hing
Aubergine	Baingan	Vangan
Bay leaf	Tej patta	Tej patta
Beetroot	Chukander	Beet
Bengal gram		
–Flour	Besan	Besan
–Husked	Chana dal	Charon ji dal
Bittergourd	Karela	Karelo
Black beans		
–Husked	Urad dal	Urad ji dal
Black pepper	Kali mirch	Kara mirch
Black salt	Kala namak	Karo loor
Brain	Bheja	Magaz
Butter		
–Clarified	Makkhan	Makkhan
Ghee	Ghee	Ghee
Cabbage	Band gobhi	Band gobhi
Capsicum	Shimla mirch	Shimla mirch
Cardamom		
–Black	Badi elaichi	Wado photo
–Green	Hari/chhoti elaichi	Photo
Carrot	Gaajar	Gaajar
Cashewnut	Kaju	Khaja
Cauliflower	Phool gobhi	Gul gobhi
Chilli		
–Dry red	Sookhi mirch	Sukho mirch
–Green	Hari mirch	Sao mirch

English	Hindi	Sindhi
–Red	Lal mirch	Gharo mirch
Cinnamon	Dalchini	Dalchini
Citric acid	Nimbu ka phool	Tatri
Cloves	Laung	Laung
Cluster beans	Gwar phalli	Guar
Coconut		
–Copra (dry)	Kopra	Suko narel
–Fresh	Nariyal	Narel
–Milk	Nariyal ka doodh	Narel jo kheer
Colocasia	Arbi	Kachalu
Coriander		
–Fresh	Hara dhania	Sava dharan
–Seeds	Sabut dhania	Sukhal dharan
Corn	Makai	Makai
Cottage cheese	Paneer	Paneer
Cream	Malai	Malai
Cucumber	Kheera/kakdi	Vango
Cumin seeds	Jeera	Jeero
–Black cumin seeds	Kala jeera/ shah jeera	Karo jeero
Curd	Dahi	Dahi
Curry leaf	Kari patta	Kari patta
Date	Khajoor	Khajoor
Egg	Anda	Bedo
Egyptian lentils		
–Husked	Masoor dal	Masoor ji dal
Fenugreek		
–Husked seeds	Methi ka dal	Methi ji dal
–Leaves	Methi bhaaji	Methi bhaaji
–Seeds	Methi dana	Hurbo
Fig	Anjeer	Anjeer
Fish	Machhi	Machhi
French bean	Fransbin	French beans
Garlic	Lassun	Thoom
Ginger		
–Fresh	Adrak	Adrak
–Dry	Saunth	Soonth
Green beans		
–Husked	Moong dal	Sai moongan ji dal
Green peas	Matar	Matar

English	Hindi	Sindhi
Jaggery	Gur	Gur
Kidney	Gurda	Gurda
Kidney beans	Rajma	Rajma
Lime	Limbu	Limo
Lotus stem	Kamal kakdi	Bhien
Mace	Javitri	Javitri
Mango	Aam	Amb
–Powder	Amchur	Amchur
Milk	Doodh	Kheer
Milo	Jowar	Jowar
–Flour	Jowar ka atta	Jowar jo atto
Mince	Keema	Kheemo
Mint	Pudina	Phudino
Mustard		
–Greens	Sarson ka saag	Rai ji bhaaji
–Husked seeds	Sarson ka dal	Rai ji dal
–Oil	Sarson ka tael	Rai jo tael
–Seeds	Sarson/rai	Rai
–Yellow	Peeli sarson	Rai ji dal
Mutton	Gosht	Teevan
Nutmeg	Jaiphal	Jaiphal
Onion	Pyaaz	Basar
Peanut	Mungphalli	Boimung
Peppercorn	Kali mirch	Kara mirch
Pigeon peas	Arhar/toover	Tuaran ji dal
Pistachio nuts	Pista	Pista
Pomegranate	Anar	Dharoo
–Seeds	Anardana	Dharoo ja dana
Pomfret	Paplet	Paplet
Poppy seeds	Khus-khus	Khus-khus
Potato	Alu	Patata
Prawn	Jhinga	Jhinga
Pumpkin		
–Red	Kaddu	Petho
Radish		
–White	Safaid muli	Muri
Rice	Chaval	Chawar
Saffron	Kesar	Kesar
Sago	Sabudana	Sabudana
Salt	Namak	Loor

English	Hindi	Sindhi
Screwpine Flower	Kewda	Kewdo
Semolina	Sooji/rava	Sooji
Sesame seed	Til	Tirr
Silver leaf	Chandi ka varq	Chandi ji warq
Sodium bicarbonate	Meetha soda	Mithi soda
Spinach	Palak	Sai bhaaji
Spring onion	Hara pyaaz	Sao basar
Sugar	Cheeni/shakkar	Khand
Sultana	Kishmish	Kishmish
Tamarind	Imli	Gidambri
Tomato	Tamatar	Tamata
Turmeric	Haldi	Haidra
Turnip	Shalgam	Gogru
Vinegar	Sirka	Sirko
Walnut	Akhrot	Akhrot
Wheat	Gehun	Karak
–Plain/refined flour	Maida	Maido
–Whole-wheat flour	Atta	Atto
Yam	Suran	Suran
Yoghurt	Substitute for curd	

Notes:

Khoya (Mawo in Sindhi): Unsweetened, dried, condensed milk made by cooking milk, stirring continuously till it forms a heavy, thick granular lump.

Kokum (kucum in Sindhi): The botanical name for kokum is *Garcina indica*. It is also called the Indian black plum and is used as a souring agent for curries in a number of Indian cuisines. Tamarind may be used as a substitute.

Index

VEGETABLES

Aubergine (Baingan):
- Masaléwara Vangan (Spicy Aubergines) 46
- Tariyal Vangan (Fried Aubergines) 48

Bittergourd (Karela):
- Bhariyal Karela (Stuffed Bittergourds) 49
- Karela Patatan mein (Bittergourds with Potatoes) 52
- Khatta Mitha Karela (Sweet and Sour Bittergourds) 50

Cauliflower:
- Masalé mein Gul Gobhi (Spicy Cauliflower) 44
- Methi mein Gul Gobhi (Cauliflower with Fenugreek Leaves) 43
- Palak mein Gul Gobhi (Cauliflower with Spinach) 45

Colocasia (Arbi):
- Kachalun ji Bhaaji (Spicy Colocasia) 56
- Tariyal Kachalu (Fried Colocasia) 57

Fenugreek Leaves (Methi):
- Methi mein Gul Gobhi (Cauliflower with Fenugreek Leaves) 43

Lotus stem (Kamal kakdi):
- Bhien jo Kheemo (Minced Lotus Stems) 55
- Bhien Patatan mein (Lotus Stems with Potatoes) 54
- Masaléwara Bhien (Spicy Lotus Stems) 53

Mixed Vegetables:
- Seyal Kofta (Vegetable Kofta in an Onion Curry) 60
- Sindhi Curry 64
- Tamatan ji Curry (Tomato Curry) 66

Okra (Bhindi):
- Bhindiyoon Basar mein (Okra with Onions) 42
- Patatan mein Bhindiyoon (Okra with Potatoes) 40
- Thoom mein Bhindiyoon (Okra with Garlic) 41

Potato:
- Bhien Patatan mein (Lotus Stems with Potatoes) 54
- Karela Patatan mein (Bittergourds with Potatoes) 52

- Koot Patata (Crisp-fried Potatoes) 51
- Patatan mein Bhindiyoon (Okra with Potatoes) 40
- Sai Bhaaji Patatan mein (Spinach with Potatoes) 63
- Saiyoon Patatan mein (Vermicelli with Potatoes) 39

Spinach:
- Kari Palak (Black Spinach) 62
- Palak mein Gul Gobhi (Cauliflower with Spinach) 45
- Sai Bhaaji (Sindhi Spinach) 58
- Sai Bhaaji Patatan mein (Spinach with Potatoes) 63

Yam:
- Suran jo Kheemo (Minced Yam) 68

The Essential Sindhi Cookbook